CliffsNotes™
Creating Web Pages with HTML

By David A. Crowder and Rhonda Crowder

IN THIS BOOK

- Create Web pages quickly and easily!
- Use color to enhance the look of your site
- Get under the hood of HTML and tweak existing Web pages
- Master the use of links
- Reinforce what you learn with CliffsNotes Review
- Find more information on creating Web pages with HTML in CliffsNotes Resour... Center and online at ʇw. cliffsnotes.com

D1005032

IDG BOOKS WORLDWIDE

IDG Books Worldwide, Inc.
An International Data Group Company
Foster City, CA • Chicago, IL • Indianapolis, IN • New York, NY

About the Author

David and Rhonda Crowder were selling hypertext systems back in the days when you had to explain what the word *hypertext* meant. Their Web site designs include the award-winning LinkFinder (www.linkfinder.com) and NetWelcome (www.netwelcome.com) sites. They have authored or coauthored over a dozen books, including *Setting Up an Internet Site for Dummies*, the bestselling *Teach Yourself the Internet*, CliffsNotes *Getting on the Internet*, and Cliffs-Notes *Shopping Online Safely*.

Publisher's Acknowledgments

Editorial

Project Editor: Jeanne S. Criswell

Acquisitions Editor: Andy Cummings

Copy Editor: Ted Cains

Technical Editors: Michael Lerch, Marita Ellixson

Special Help: Shelley Lea

Production

Indexer: York Production Services, Inc.

Proofreader: York Production Services, Inc.

IDG Books Indianapolis Production Department

CliffsNotes™ Creating Web Pages with HTML

Published by
IDG Books Worldwide, Inc.
An International Data Group Company
919 E. Hillsdale Blvd.
Suite 400
Foster City, CA 94404
www.idgbooks.com (IDG Books Worldwide Web site)
www.cliffsnotes.com (CliffsNotes Web site)

Distributed in the United States by IDG Books Worldwide, Inc.

Distributed by CDG Books Canada Inc. for Canada; by Transworld Publishers Limited in the United Kingdom; by IDG Norge Books for Norway; by IDG Sweden Books for Sweden; by IDG Books Australia Publishing Corporation Pty. Ltd. for Australia and New Zealand; by TransQuest Publishers Pte Ltd. for Singapore, Malaysia, Thailand, Indonesia, and Hong Kong; by Gotop Information Inc. for Taiwan; by ICG Muse, Inc. for Japan; by Intersoft for South Africa; by Eyrolles for France; by International Thomson Publishing for Germany, Austria and Switzerland; by Distribuidora Cuspide for Argentina; by LR International for Brazil; by Galileo Libros for Chile; by Ediciones ZETA S.C.R. Ltda. for Peru; by WS Computer Publishing Corporation, Inc., for the Philippines; by Contemporanea de Ediciones for Venezuela; by Express Computer Distributors for the Caribbean and West Indies; by Micronesia Media Distributor, Inc. for Micronesia; by Chips Computadoras S.A. de C.V. for Mexico; by Editorial Norma de Panama S.A. for Panama; by American Bookshops for Finland.

For general information on IDG Books Worldwide's books in the U.S., please call our Consumer Customer Service department at **800-762-2974**. For reseller information, including discounts and premium sales, please call our Reseller Customer Service department at **800-434-3422**.

For information on where to purchase IDG Books Worldwide's books outside the U.S., please contact our International Sales department at 317-596-5530 or fax **317-596-5692**.

For consumer information on foreign language translations, please contact our Customer Service department at **1-800-434-3422**, fax 317-596-5692, or e-mail rights@idgbooks.com.

For information on licensing foreign or domestic rights, please phone **+1-650-655-3109**.

For sales inquiries and special prices for bulk quantities, please contact our Sales department at 650-655-3200 or write to the address above.

For information on using IDG Books Worldwide's books in the classroom or for ordering examination copies, please contact our Educational Sales department at **800-434-2086** or fax 317-596-5499.

For press review copies, author interviews, or other publicity information, please contact our Public Relations department at 650-655-3000 or fax **650-655-3299**.

For authorization to photocopy items for corporate, personal, or educational use, please contact Copyright Clearance Center, 222 Rosewood Drive, Danvers, MA 01923, or fax **978-750-4470**.

Table of Contents

INTRODUCTION

HTML, or *Hypertext Markup Language*, defines how a Web browser interprets and formats a Web page. While many Web page authors create content in a program such as Microsoft FrontPage Express, which creates the code behind the scenes for you, exploring HTML can help you see how Web pages work. You can then use HTML to create a Web page or to enhance and tweak practically any existing page, even if you created it in a Web page layout program.

Throughout this book, we guide you through creating a set of three Web pages (a basic genealogy site for the fictitious Brown family) to show you how HTML works. You can either replicate the example site or create one of your own. In any event, this book launches you into the exciting world of HTML.

Why Do You Need This Book?

Can you answer yes to any of these questions?

- Do you need to learn HTML fast?
- Don't have time to read 500 pages about HTML?
- Do you want to get "under the hood" of your Web page?
- Do you need to use HTML to tweak your existing Web page?

If so, then CliffsNotes *Creating Web Pages with HTML* is for you!

How to Use This Book

You can read this book straight through or just look for the information you need. You can find information on a particular topic in a number of ways: You can search the index in the back of the book, locate your topic in the Table of Contents, or read the In This Chapter list in each chapter. To reinforce your learning, check out the Review and Resource Center at the back of the book. To help you find important information in the book, look for the following icons in the text:

If you see a Remember icon, make a mental note of this text — it's worth keeping in mind.

If you see a Tip icon, you know that you've run across a helpful hint, uncovered a secret, or received good advice.

The Warning icon alerts you to something that could be dangerous, requires special caution, or should be avoided.

Don't Miss Our Web Site

Keep up with the intriguing world of the Internet by visiting our Web site at www.cliffsnotes.com. Here's what you find:

- Interactive tools that are fun and informative
- Links to interesting Web sites
- Additional resources to help you continue your learning

At www.cliffsnotes.com, you can even register for a new feature called CliffsNotes Daily, which offers you newsletters on a variety of topics, delivered right to your e-mail inbox each business day.

See you at www.cliffsnotes.com!

CHAPTER 1
CREATING A BASIC WEB PAGE

IN THIS CHAPTER

- Building the framework
- Understanding HTML elements and tags

In this chapter, we cover everything you need to know about putting together the framework for a basic Web page. In addition to showing you how *HTML* (or *Hypertext Markup Language* — the computer language that makes documents for the World Wide Web) works, we have a little bit of fun along the way. During the course of this book, we develop a Web site that actually applies the material to a "real world" solution — the Brown family history site. The only difference between this site and a site you may actually create is that the Brown family is a figment of our imaginations.

The location of a file, by the way, is called a *URL* (or *Uniform Resource Locator*). URLs are the addresses of files and are key to the Hypertext Markup Language's functionality. Without URLs, HTML would be nothing more than a method for laying out text. You can link a page to another file by specifying the URL as an attribute of certain HTML elements. This capability is what makes the "Hypertext" in HTML possible. You can find more details on URLs in Chapter 5.

We encourage you to do what we do throughout the book, either by replicating our sample site or creating an original site of your own. That's the best way to discover the ins and outs of HTML.

Assembling Your Tools

You don't need a lot of expensive software or hardware to create your own Web pages in HTML. In fact, you probably don't need much more than the equipment you already use to browse the Web. Just make sure you have the following:

- **A text editor:** You can create and edit Web pages in any text editor. Notepad, which comes with Windows 95/98/NT, works just fine, as does SimpleText, which comes with the Mac OS. You can also use Microsoft Word or Corel WordPerfect — just make sure that, if you use one of these word processing programs, you save your file in plain-text format.

  The good news about formatting text and images with HTML is that the procedure is pretty much the same as adding and manipulating text for documents in a text editor or word processing program. If you're at all familiar with either type of program, you'll feel right at home.

- **A Web browser:** In order to preview your Web pages (that is, view them in a browser window before they go online), you need a Web browser. In Chapter 8, you work with a special way of dividing and organizing Web pages called frames, so you need a browser that supports frames. Netscape Navigator 2.0 or later and Microsoft Internet Explorer 3.0 or later support frames; we recommend using the latest version of each.

You may want to test your Web pages in both browsers, because each browser handles HTML a little differently and each is widely popular (about a 50-50 split between users, as of this writing). Both browsers are free to download and use. Just go to www.netscape.com or www.microsoft.com. If you don't believe us when we say that the browsers differ, then jump to Chapter 6 on tables to see the differences in action!

■ **A modem and Internet connection:** Unless you intend to make your Web pages available only on an internal network, such as an office network, you need a way to connect to the Internet and an account with an Internet service provider (ISP). Most computers these days come with modems and a way to sign up with an ISP.

These points cover the basics you need. Now, you can roll up your virtual sleeves and get to work!

If you plan to create or edit your own Web page images, you need a scanner or other device to capture the graphics in the form of a computer file. You also need an image-editing program, such as Paint Shop Pro (www.jasc.com), to edit the files. Working with images in this way is beyond the scope of this book, but you can find some next-step resources in the CliffsNotes Resource Center at the end of this book.

Building the Framework

The basic Web page you create here can serve as a template for just about everything you ever do on the Web. This Web page has only four HTML commands or instructions (or as they are called throughout this book, *elements*), but the page's structure is the basic skeleton for any Web page.

Starting a Web page

You use your text editor or word processing program to create HTML files. An *HTML file* is a plain-text file that a Web browser translates into a graphical representation of a Web page. The *source code* (programmerese for the instructions that make up an HTML file) that you create for a particular Web page is the same in every program. However, depending on which program you use, the process of saving the file may be different. If you're using a program dedicated to making Web pages, the program automatically understands how to handle this process. On the other hand, a plain-text editor often insists on using the file extension .txt when you save a file created in it, and a word processing program usually tries to save a file in its own proprietary format (such as .doc or .wpd). You need to make sure that you not only save the file as a plain-text file, but that you also have the program give the file the extension .htm (or .html). Most modern word processing programs have an option to save the file as an HTML file.

If you're using a word processing program and it doesn't have an option for saving a document as an HTML file, look for words such as *text file, ASCII, plain text,* or *text only* in your save options.

To make your first Web page, follow these steps:

1. Open your text editor.

2. Type the following lines:

```
<HTML>

<HEAD>
<TITLE>Brown Family Home Page</TITLE>
</HEAD>

<BODY>
<H1>The Brown Family Home Page</H1>
</BODY>

</HTML>
```

Don't worry if you don't know what all this HTML mumbo-jumbo means; we get to that in a moment. Just be sure that you enter the less-than (<) and greater-than (>) angle brackets, as shown, and that you don't add any blank spaces between these symbols and the commands (HTML, HEAD, BODY, H1) and sometimes the slash (/) inside them.

3. Save the file, naming it main.htm.

The H1 element, by the way, creates a major heading (called a Heading 1). You find out how to use headings in Chapter 2.

Search engines are special programs that scan the World Wide Web to make listings of Web pages for sites like Webcrawler and Excite! A search engine may use the content of the TITLE element to name your Web page in its listings. So be sure to give all your pages good, descriptive titles that accurately identify the pages' contents for potential viewers.

Viewing your Web page

The HTML code that you typed in the previous section looks pretty boring in your word processing program. But you can see what the page looks like on the Web by viewing the page in a Web browser. To do so, just open the file in your Web browser. In either Netscape Navigator or Microsoft Internet Explorer, follow these steps:

1. Launch your Web browser.

2. Choose File⇨Open Page (in Navigator) or File⇨Open (in Internet Explorer).

3. In the dialog box that appears (see Figure 1-1), enter the location and filename, or just click Choose File (in Navigator) or Browse (in Internet Explorer) to locate the file on your hard drive.

Figure 1-1:   Opening an HTML file in Netscape Navigator.

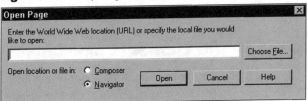

4. Click Open (in Navigator) or OK (in Internet Explorer).

Figure 1-2 shows what your HTML file looks like in a Web browser.

Figure 1-2: Your Web page as it appears in Internet Explorer.

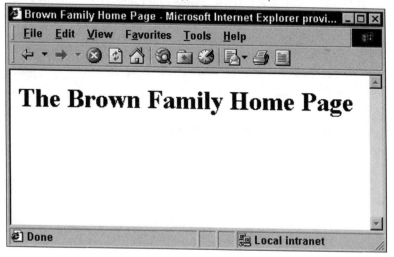

You may want to keep your Web browser open while you're editing an HTML document so that you can flip back and forth between the browser and your text editor. This way, you can immediately see how your changes affect the Web page's appearance in the browser. However, before you can see those changes, you must save the HTML document in the text editor. (Usually, choosing File⇨Save gets the job done.) Then all you have to do is switch to the browser and click Reload (in Navigator) or Refresh (in Internet Explorer) to see the changes to the page.

Understanding HTML Elements and Tags

The text you typed into your text editor is the source code of the Web page. The source code is composed of simple instructions called *elements*. Each element has a particular function in describing one portion of the document.

A Web browser decides exactly how it interprets an element. HTML suggests but doesn't control the interpretation. To make sure that your Web page appears exactly the way you want it to, always view it in whatever browser(s) you think visitors may use.

Each element has a *start tag* and, usually but not always, an *end tag*. The start and end tags are always identical, except for the forward slash in the end tag, which is how you tell the difference. The tags include the name of the element, which usually clearly describes its function. The material between the start and end tags is called the *content*. For example, the following TITLE element has as its content the title of your Web page:

```
<TITLE>Brown Family Home Page</TITLE>
```

A tag is not the same thing as an element. The element is everything from the start tag through the end tag, including not only the content, but also the tags themselves.

Tags are always denoted by angle brackets (< and >), which tell a Web browser that the material between the brackets is a markup instruction and shouldn't be displayed on the Web page. Thus, in the example TITLE element, a Web browser knows that "Brown Family Home Page" is the title of the Web page and the only part of the element that should appear in the browser's title bar.

Understanding the container relationship

HTML is based on a *container relationship*, which means that, with one exception, each element is contained within another one. Look again at the code for your Web page:

```
<HTML>

<HEAD>
<TITLE>Brown Family Home Page</TITLE>
</HEAD>

<BODY>
<H1>The Brown Family Home Page</H1>
</BODY>

</HTML>
```

As you can see, the exception to the container relationship is the HTML element; it's the outer limit. The HTML element encompasses everything on the page, visible or not. Within it, the HEAD element contains informational material that is not displayed on the actual Web page; in this case, the TITLE element. The BODY element, which also falls within the HTML element, contains everything on the page that is visible within a Web browser, such as the H1 element.

Exploring attributes

In addition to content, elements can also have *attributes*. Attributes are always found within the start tag of the element, and they tell a Web browser how the following content should be affected. Common attributes include such features as color, height, width, or the location of a linked file. An attribute is associated with an HTML element by an equals sign (=) and quotation marks, like this:

```
<H1 align="center">The Brown Family Home
Page</H1>
```

In this example, `align` is an attribute of the H1 heading element, and `"center"` tells a Web browser to center the heading on the page. You discover more about aligning text elements, such as headings, in Chapter 3.

Be sure not to insert any extra blank spaces when using attributes, or a Web browser won't display your page correctly. An attribute is separated from an element by a *single* blank space. *No* blank spaces appear around the equals sign or quotation marks. Also, the quotation marks have to be straight up-and-down *double primes* rather than the curly quotes used by many word processing programs. If you use Notepad as your HTML editor, the program adds double primes automatically.

The *value* of an attribute is the term that follows the equals sign and that is enclosed in quotation marks. The value determines what actually happens as a result of the setting. For example, setting the `color` attribute for text to red obviously has a different result than setting it to blue.

Like elements, attributes generally have names that clearly indicate their function and are easy to understand. For example, `bgcolor` is the background color attribute, `width` sets the width of an element, `align` sets the alignment, and so on.

You can add two or more attributes to a single element by separating each one with a single blank space. For example, the following HTML code is for a *horizontal rule*, a straight line across the Web page represented by the HR element:

```
<HR width="67%" size="6" align="center">
```

The start tag is all you have in this case; because the horizontal rule itself can have no content, no end tag is necessary. Within the start tag, you find the name of the element followed by the attributes for its width on the page, size (line thickness), and alignment on the page. This horizontal rule takes up two-thirds of the page's width, is 6 pixels thick, and is centered on the page.

Traditionally, elements are typed in capital letters, while attributes and their values are typed in lowercase letters. This method makes the source code more readable and its parts easier to identify at a glance. However, you don't have to follow this convention; HTML is not case sensitive.

If you don't specify the value of an attribute, the browser displays the *default value* for the element. Default values vary from element to element, of course. The HR element with no attributes looks like this:

```
<HR>
```

In this code, the default value of the `width` attribute for the HR element is 100 percent of the page width, and the default value of the `align` attribute is center alignment. The default value of the `size` attribute (the line thickness) is not defined in the HTML specification, which means that the browser decides the value for you. So not specifying attributes for the HR element is exactly the same as the following:

```
<HR width="100%" align="center">
```

Understanding element levels

Elements that cause a new line to be started on a Web page are called *block-level elements*. Elements that can reside within an existing line without making a new line are called *inline elements*. For example, the P (for *paragraph*) element starts a new paragraph, and a new paragraph obviously requires a new line for itself. So the element is a block-level element. The I (for *italic*) element, on the other hand, simply makes the text within its tags italic and doesn't require a new line. So the I element is an inline element.

Because most inline elements are embedded within a line of text and used for modifying text, they're also sometimes called *text-level elements*.

Combining HTML elements

When you have two HTML elements enclosing a single object (some text or a graphic), which element goes inside or outside the other element doesn't matter. For example, the following two lines of HTML have the same result:

```
<H1><I>This Is a Level-1 Heading</I></H1>
<I><H1>This Is a Level-1 Heading</H1></I>
```

In either case, the words *This Is a Level-1 Heading* are displayed as a level-1 heading and are in italics. The important thing is to keep both the start tag and the end tag of one HTML element in the same place with relation to the other HTML element. Avoid the following:

```
<H1><I>This Is a Level-1 Heading</H1></I>
```

Mixing HTML elements this way can confuse a Web browser, and it won't display your text the way you want.

At this point, take a deep breath and pat yourself on the back: You've assembled your Web page toolkit and created the framework for your first HTML document. Bear in mind that you can use this framework to build any Web page you desire. In the next chapter, you add text to the Web page and format that text to give it life. As you progress through the book, what you discover about tinkering directly with the HTML source code can also help you see ways to enhance preexisting Web pages created in an HTML editor or Web publishing program, such as Microsoft FrontPage Express or Adobe PageMill. Even though such programs create the HTML code for the user, their capabilities vary, and sometimes you just have to know how to get under the hood!

CHAPTER 2

ADDING AND MANIPULATING TEXT

IN THIS CHAPTER

- Adding text to your Web page
- Using heading elements
- Adding color to text
- Setting inline styles
- Changing font sizes and faces
- Handling special characters

Web pages are mostly composed of words, so you shouldn't be surprised that, in this chapter, we show you how to add text to your Web page and then change the look of that text in HTML. You have heading elements, which are block-level elements that automatically set all the text in a line to a particular size. Then you have several inline elements that let you determine the look of the text, right down to the level of individual characters. (Remember block-level and inline elements from Chapter 1? If not, go back for a quick refresher.) Your choices include text size and other characteristics, such as bold, italic, or color. And HTML has a set of codes that enable you to display special characters that aren't even on your keyboard.

Adding Text to Your Web Page

Before you can learn to manipulate text, you must have some text to work with. When entering text into an HTML document, just follow the same word processing conventions that you're accustomed to when working with a program like Microsoft Word. However, you need to keep a few things in mind when working in HTML.

Unlike your favorite word processing program, HTML doesn't recognize when you hit the Enter key at the end of a paragraph. That's why you have to use the P element to separate paragraphs. HTML doesn't allow you to indent the first line of a new paragraph, which is why the P element places a full line space between paragraphs. That's the same as hitting the Enter key twice after a paragraph in Microsoft Word. The line space simply makes the paragraphs easier to read.

That's not to say that you can't use the Enter key when typing HTML. In fact, we recommend that you hit Enter at the end of a line of HTML to make the code easier to read (just like we did in the code examples in Chapter 1). Also, you can hit the Enter key as many times as you want; your browser won't know the difference when it interprets your Web document.

The P element has an optional end tag. You can end your paragraphs with a `</P>` tag, but it's not required and rarely used.

What if you want to create an extra blank space between paragraphs, though? (For example, a two- or three-line break between paragraphs that doesn't have any content.) The P element does create a single blank line between paragraphs, but sometimes you need additional space. One of the quirks of the P element is that it must have content. Empty P elements, such as the one shown in the following code snippet, are not allowed in HTML:

```
<P>This is the first paragraph.
<P>This is the second paragraph.
<P>
<P>This is the third paragraph.
```

The result, when displayed, appears as if the empty P element weren't there at all.

The way to get around this situation is to give the P element some invisible content. Unfortunately, you can't just use the blank space you get by hitting the spacebar, but you can use the following special code to insert two blank spaces:

```
<P> 
```

For a single additional blank space, use the BR line break element as follows:

```
<BR> 
```

Using two `<BR> ` commands is the same as using a single `<P> ` command.

Make sure that you don't drop the semicolon at the end of that code, or you end up with the characters * * showing up on your Web page.

When you insert the HTML line break element, BR, you break one line and start a new one. The BR element doesn't add a blank space in either of the two major Web browsers — Netscape Navigator or Microsoft Internet Explorer. You may want to use the BR element when you want to force a word to the next line without creating a new paragraph.

To add some text to your Web page, follow these steps:

1. In your open HTML document (main.htm), type the following lines below the H1 element and before the `</BODY>` tag. (Keep in mind that you can replicate the sample Web site's text, which we provide here, or substitute your own text.)

```
<P>Welcome to the Brown Family Web site. In
the following pages, we celebrate the story of
```

```
Samuel and Honoria Brown and their
descendants. The main areas of the site are
described below.
<P>Visit the Brown Family Links page to find
out about other families who are related to
the Browns.
<P>If you're related to the Brown family, you
can list your family by filling out the form
on the Register Your Family page.
```

2. Save the file, keeping the name main.htm.

3. Display the Web page in your browser.

Figure 2-1 shows the results. Now you have some text to work with.

Figure 2-1:   Adding text to your Web page.

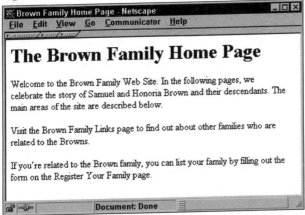

Using Heading Elements

A *heading* is a word or phrase that you highlight with bold-face or some other distinctive type style to distinguish it from the body text. Headings "point the way" to important parts of a page.

In HTML, you can choose from six different sizes of headings. Consequently, you may see heading elements referred to as the H*x* elements, because they all start with an H followed by a number from 1 to 6. The H1 element is the largest; the H6 element is the smallest. H1 elements usually signal main topics, H2 elements subtopics of H1 elements, H3 sub-subtopics, and so on. You rarely get down to the H4, H5, and H6 levels.

To illustrate how heading elements work, add some level-2 (H2) subheadings to the opening page of the Brown Family Web site by following these steps:

1. Type a new subheading, **Brown Family Links**, just above the paragraph that begins "Visit the Brown Family Links page . . ." and then place <H2> . . . </H2> tags around it, like this:

   ```
   <H2>Brown Family Links</H2>
   ```

2. Type a second subheading, **Register Your Family**, just above the paragraph that begins "If you're related to the Brown family . . ." and then place <H2> . . . </H2> tags around it, like this:

   ```
   <H2>Register Your Family</H2>
   ```

   The HTML code should look like this:

   ```
   <HTML>

   <HEAD>
   <TITLE>Brown Family Home Page</TITLE>
   </HEAD>

   <BODY>
   <H1>The Brown Family Home Page</H1>
   <P>Welcome to the Brown Family Web site. In
   the following pages, we celebrate the story of
   ```

```
Samuel and Honoria Brown and their
descendants. The main areas of the site are
described below.
<H2>Brown Family Links</H2>
<P>Visit the Brown Family Links page to find
out about other families who are related to
the Browns.
<H2>Register Your Family</H2>
<P>If you're related to the Brown family, you
can list your family by filling out the form
on the Register Your Family page.
</BODY>

</HTML>
```

3. Save the file.

4. Display the Web page in your browser. Figure 2-2 shows the result.

Figure 2-2:   Using heading elements.

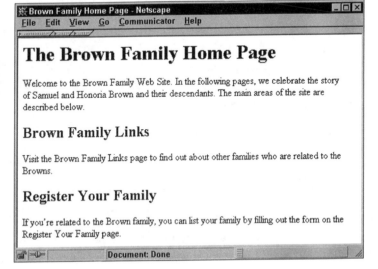

Making Your Text Colorful

One of the best things about Web pages is that you can play with the colors used in them. By default, Web pages have plain white backgrounds with black text — about as dull as it gets. But as HTML has grown more sophisticated, color has become a regular and expected feature of Web pages.

You can specify colors either by a name or by a numeric code, which is called *hexadecimal* (or *hex*, for short). Hexadecimal codes (for example, #FF0000 for red) give you the ability to specify millions of colors. However, for the purpose of creating your Web page, you may want to limit your palette somewhat. For that reason, don't worry about hexadecimal codes, which can be very complicated. Instead, use standard color names. Table 2-1 shows just a few of the names you can use for each color.

Table 2-1: HTML Color Names

aqua	aquamarine	beige	black
blue	blueviolet	brown	cyan
green	greenyellow	hotpink	indianred
maroon	mediumblue	mediumpurple	medium turquoise
medium violetred	midnightblue	navy	olive
pink	plum	powderblue	purple
red	royalblue	salmon	sandybrown
turquoise	violet	white	yellow

Table 2-1 lists only a few of the standard color designations that Web browsers can interpret and display. As HTML evolves, the list of possible color names grows dramatically. A nice chart that shows the colors that correspond to each name can be found at www.inter-linked.com/color-chart.html.

The HTML color names should give you a rich enough palette to work with. But if you want access to the millions of colors you can specify, you may want to use a color picker to visually choose the colors and get their proper hexadecimal codes. You can find any number of freeware or shareware color pickers. See the Resource Center at the end of the book for more information.

You can use color in your Web page in a variety of ways. For example, you can change your page's background color. To do so, you add the attribute bgcolor to the <BODY> tag. (Be sure to separate BODY and bgcolor with a single blank space.) You can also change the color of your Web page's headings, subheadings, or any other text. To do so, you enclose the text in the <FONT>...</FONT> tags and add the attribute color to the FONT element.

Use named colors to set the color of your Web page's background, headings, and subheadings by following these steps:

1. In your open HTML file (main.htm), modify the BODY element by adding bgcolor, the equals sign (=), and the standard HTML color name enclosed in quotation marks. Specify beige as the sample Web page's background color. After you do so, the HTML code looks like this:

```
<BODY bgcolor="beige">
```

2. Change the font color of the level-1 heading by enclosing the text in the HTML tags <FONT>...</FONT> and add the attribute color to the FONT element. Because the standard HTML color name rosybrown looks good against the beige background you added in Step 1, modify the heading at the top of the sample Web page so that the HTML code looks like this:

```
<H1><FONT color="rosybrown">The Brown Family
Home Page</FONT></H1>
```

3. Repeat Step 2 for the subheadings. After you make the sample Web page's subheadings rosybrown, to match the level-1 heading, the resulting HTML code looks like this:

```
<H2><FONT color="rosybrown">Brown Family
Links</FONT></H2>
<H2><FONT color="rosybrown">Register Your
Family</FONT></H2>
```

Remember

The color of an element is one of its attributes. So bgcolor is an attribute of the BODY element and sets its background color; color is an attribute of the H1 and FONT elements and sets their text color. The colors themselves, beige and rosybrown, are values of the respective attributes.

4. Save the file.

5. Display the Web page in your browser.

Although Figure 2-3 is in black and white, you can still get an idea of the results.

Figure 2-3: Adding color to the Web page's background and text.

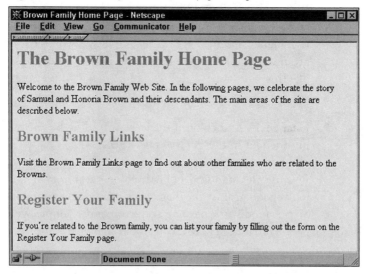

Different font colors display better or worse depending on how much they contrast with the background color. This characteristic is a key factor in Web page design. Try setting the text color to the same color as the background — the text disappears. The more two colors resemble one another, the less distinctive they are; the less they resemble one another, the more distinctive they are.

Take a bit of time to try different background and font color combinations.

Setting Inline Styles

You can use several different inline elements in HTML to control the appearance of fonts. All you have to do is bracket the text you want to affect with the appropriate tags. Thus, to make a word italic, you put it between <I> and </I> tags, like so:

```
<P>This is some <I>italic</I> lettering.
```

The two most commonly used types of inline styles are italic and bold. You format bold in the same manner as italic, except that the affected text is placed between <B> and </B> tags. Some less common text styles include strikethrough and underline. Strikethrough text is normal text with a line drawn through the middle of it. You can use either the <STRIKE>...</STRIKE> or the <S>...</S> tags to format strikethrough text.

Underlined text, which falls between <U> and </U> tags, causes a special problem on Web pages. Using underlined text on Web pages can confuse visitors because links to other pages are automatically underlined. For this reason, avoiding the U element is best. Use italics or bold to emphasize words or phrases.

To see what bold and italic text styles look like in a Web browser, modify your Web page by following these steps:

1. In the first paragraph, place `<I>...</I>` and `<B>...</B>` tags around the text you want to affect. In The Brown Family Home Page, for example, place `<I>...</I>` tags around "The Brown Family Web Site" and `<B>...</B>` tags around "Samuel and Honoria Brown," like so:

```
<P>Welcome to <I>The Brown Family Web
Site</I>. In the following pages, we celebrate
the story of <B>Samuel and Honoria Brown</B>
and their descendants. The main areas of the
site are described below.
```

2. Save the file.

3. Display the Web page in your browser. Figure 2-4 shows the result.

Figure 2-4: Bold and italic text styles.

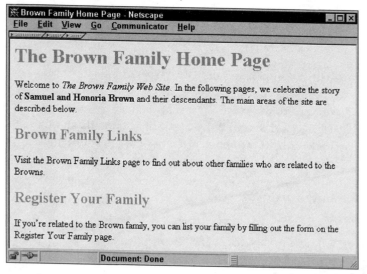

The Brown Family Home Page

Welcome to *The Brown Family Web Site*. In the following pages, we celebrate the story of **Samuel and Honoria Brown** and their descendants. The main areas of the site are described below.

Brown Family Links

Visit the Brown Family Links page to find out about other families who are related to the Browns.

Register Your Family

If you're related to the Brown family, you can list your family by filling out the form on the Register Your Family page.

Don't bother using the B element on the text in a heading element because all heading elements are already bold. Using code such as `<H1><B>Heading</B></H1>` does nothing.

Changing Font Sizes and Faces

Earlier in this chapter, you discover how to use the FONT element to set the color of the text it encloses. The FONT element can also set the look and size of that text.

Understanding font sizes

The font size for normal text is arbitrarily designated as 3, on a scale of 1 to 7. Font sizes work in exactly the opposite way that heading sizes do; the smallest font size is 1 and the largest is 7. The six heading element sizes are the same as the first six font sizes, but in reverse order. As a result, an H1 heading is font size 6, an H2 heading is font size 5, an H3 heading is font size 4, and so on until you reach the H6 heading, which is a font size 1.

Heading elements smaller than H3 are almost never used on Web pages. Because the default font size is 3 and an H4 heading font size is 3, the H4 heading fails to stand out from the size 3 body text under it.

When you become proficient with formatting Web pages, be sure to look into Cascading Style Sheets (CSS), which provide you with a powerful means to format not only a single Web page but many pages on the same site. With CSS, you can specify an exact font size. However, power on the Web is always in the hands of the user, and users can override your style sheet with one of their own.

Specifying font sizes

HTML has two different ways to specify font sizes. One is with a specific size number, while the other is relative to the default size. With the first technique, you simply state at which size the lettering should appear. With the relative technique, you give a positive number for a larger size or a negative number for a smaller size.

The other approach to assigning relative sizes to fonts — the BIG and SMALL elements — is almost never used because simply assigning a numerical value is much easier. But if you want to, you can use these elements. For example, the following lines of code are equivalent in their effect:

```
<P>This is normal size.
<P><FONT size="4">This is one size larger than
normal.</FONT>
<P><FONT size="+1">And so is this one.</FONT>
<P><BIG>And this one is, too.</BIG>
```

The default font size is 3.

By the way, you can't make a font smaller than size 1 or larger than size 7 by assigning a relative value. For example, you won't end up with a size 9 if you try to set the font to +6. You get the maximum of 7. Likewise, using a -7 won't give you a font size of -4. Instead, you get the minimum of 1.

Changing faces

Font faces are the actual appearance of the lettering. Arial, Times New Roman, and Courier are three of the most commonly used faces on the Web and are likely to be on any user's computer, whether the computer is running Windows, the Mac OS, or UNIX.

So far, all the text on The Brown Family Home Page has been in the Times New Roman font. Times New Roman is part of the *serif* font family, meaning that the letters have ornaments on the ends that make them more readable. Serifs, theoretically, help readers recognize letters more easily. Serifs also are irresistible to most font artists.

Opposed to the serif font family is the *sans serif* font family (or for all you French majors out there, "without serif"). Common examples of sans serif fonts are Arial, Helvetica,

Verdana, and Swiss. These letters are composed of simpler straight lines. While serif fonts are normally used for the main text in books and magazines, sans serif fonts are used for headings and article titles.

Another type of font face is *monospace*. The characters in monospace fonts are all the same width, like the characters on an old typewriter. The code that you see in this book is in the monospace font Courier. Monospace fonts can be either serif or sans serif.

Tip

You don't know what kind of computer system visitors to your Web site may use. Therefore, listing more than one of the common font names is customary, which helps to ensure that the users see more or less exactly what you intend. If users don't have the listed font on their systems, the Web browser has to make an educated guess about which font is the closest match. Giving several options makes getting an exact match more likely. The last alternative in such a listing is to simply list the font family.

To view different font faces, change the headings on your home page by following these steps:

1. Enclose the specified text with <FONT face>...
</FONT> tags and provide several options (such as Arial, Helvetica, and the generic sans serif) as attributes of the FONT element. For this book's ongoing example, add a second attribute to the FONT element to define the color as rosybrown, like so:

```
<H1><FONT color="rosybrown" face="Arial,
Helvetica, sans-serif">The The Brown Family
Home Page</FONT></H1>
```

Notice that between the words sans and serif a hyphen is required because, in HTML code, a space indicates the end of one command and the start of another.

2. Repeat Step 1 for the subheadings on your home page. Adjust the code for the two subheadings in the ongoing example like so:

```
<H2><FONT color="rosybrown" face="Arial,
Helvetica, sans-serif">Brown Family
Links</FONT></H2>
<H2><FONT color="rosybrown" face="Arial,
Helvetica, sans-serif">Register Your
Family</FONT></H2>
```

You practice changing the font size of text later in this chapter.

3. Save the file.

4. Display the Web page in your browser. Figure 2-5 shows the results.

Figure 2-5: Changing the font face.

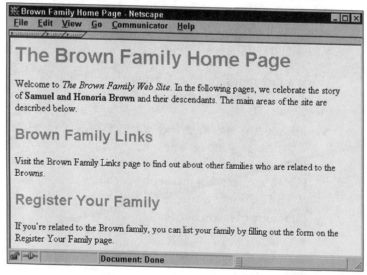

Inserting Special Characters

Sometimes, you may need to have a character that isn't available on your keyboard, such as the copyright symbol. Or suppose, for example, that you need to display actual HTML code on your Web page because you want to put together a tutorial on HTML. If you type the HTML code in the normal way, visitors' browsers interpret the tags rather than display them. So you have a real problem.

Fortunately, you can bypass the normal character entry methods and use codes for special characters. These codes are called *character entity references*. Far too many exist to list in this book, but you can find a complete listing on the World Wide Web Consortium's Web site at `www.w3.org/TR/REC-html40/sgml/entities.html`.

Practically every letter or symbol you could want is included in the listings, from all the sigmas and kappas for fraternity and sorority folks to things such as yens and pounds for those who indulge in international finance. Table 2-2 shows some of the more commonly useful ones.

Table 2-2: Some Useful Character Codes

Character	Code
Cent	&cent;
Copyright	&copy;
Degrees	&deg;
Euro	&euro;
Greater Than	&gt;
Less Than	&lt;
Nonbreaking Space	
Plus or Minus	&plusmn;
Pound	&pound;
Trademark (reg)	&reg;
Yen	&yen;

Tip

When you want to display HTML code on a Web page, all you have to do is use the Less Than (`&lt;`) and Greater Than (`&gt;`) symbols in place of the left and right angle brackets in the code.

You can use the standard `&copy` character code to add a copyright symbol (©) to a Web page. You may also want to put the copyright notice in italic (with `<I>...</I>` tags) to show that it's different from the main text. To accomplish these things on the example home page, just follow these steps:

1. Add the following line between the last paragraph and the `</BODY>` tag:

```
<P><I>&copy; 2020 The Brown Foundation.</I>
```

2. Save the file.

3. Display the Web page in your browser. Figure 2-6 shows the result.

Figure 2-6: The copyright notice.

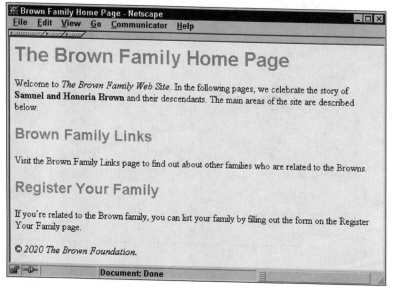

You must always use the ampersand (&) to start a character code and a semicolon (;) to end it. That's the character code equivalent of start and end tags, and if you don't include them, a Web browser won't recognize the special characters for what they are.

Changing Font Size

The viewer's Web browser controls the default size of Web page text. Some browsers are set to display Web page body text in 12-point Times New Roman, others in 10-point Helvetica, and so on.

You can enclose selected text with `<FONT size="n">...</FONT>` tags to ensure that Web browsers display that text in a particular size. Or you can use "-1" or "+1", for example, to make the text slightly smaller or larger than the surrounding text. In the example home page, you can format the copyright notice as smaller-than-normal size (so that the notice resembles fine print) by following these steps:

1. Scroll down to the copyright notice you added to the example home page in the previous section and modify the HTML code as follows:

```
<P><I><FONT size="-1">&copy; 2020 The Brown
Foundation.</FONT></I>
```

2. Save the file.

3. Display the Web page in your browser.

As you can see, HTML is great for formatting individual words, phrases, and sentences. You can also use HTML for controlling paragraphs and other blocks of text by specifying where they should align and break, as you discover in the next chapter.

CHAPTER 3

FORMATTING WEB PAGES

IN THIS CHAPTER

- Aligning elements
- Adding horizontal rules
- Using lists

While heading elements (see Chapter 2) provide some degree of formatting for Web pages, a number of other approaches can turn a plain Web page into something much more exciting.

Alignment of text and images, plus the use of dividing lines called *horizontal rules,* are two of the more common approaches to Web page formatting. HTML also offers different types of lists that prove useful in structuring the layout of information. In this chapter, you discover how to use all of them.

Aligning Elements

Many HTML elements have an `align` attribute that sets how the element aligns on the Web page. However, the implementation of this attribute is inconsistent. For example, the IMG (image) element has no center alignment.

You can set the `align` attribute of text elements (H1, H2, H3, H4, H5, H6, and P) to a value of left, center, right, or justify. Here's what each of those values means:

- Left-aligned text is flush with the left margin and is ragged on the right side.

- Center-aligned text has each line spaced an equal distance from both margins.

- Right-aligned text is flush with the right margin and is ragged on the left side.

- Justified text is flush with both margins.

By default, any block-level element is left-aligned, so you don't have to do anything to make these elements left-aligned. If the element is aligned in some other way, you can return it to left alignment by specifically setting its `align` attribute to a value of left or by deleting the `align` attribute entirely.

To see how various alignments look in your Web browser, add another Web page to the Brown Family site by following these steps:

1. Open your text editor.

2. Type the following code:

```
<HTML>

<HEAD>
<TITLE>Brown Family Links</TITLE>
</HEAD>

<BODY bgcolor="beige">

<H1 align="center"><FONT color="rosybrown"
face="Arial, Helvetica, sans-serif">Brown
Family Links</FONT></H1>

<P><I>With all beings and all things, we shall
be as relatives.</I>
<BR>—Sioux Indian saying

<P align="justify">Descendants of Sam and
Honoria Brown live all over the United States.
Do you belong to one of the branches of the
```

```
family? The links below lead you to branches
that we've documented. Two of Sam and
Honoria's children survived into adulthood.

<P>Smith Family Web Page
<P>Jones Family Web Page
<P>Doe Family Web Page

</BODY>

</HTML>
```

3. Save the file as links.htm.

4. Display the Web page in your browser. Figure 3-1 shows the result.

Figure 3-1: The second page of your Web site.

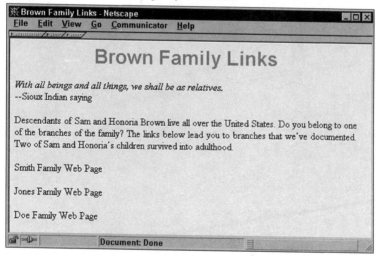

The preceding example uses the <BR> line break tag after the quotation. Use <BR> instead of <P> before a line of text when you want to separate it from the preceding line without inserting a blank space between the two lines. After you view Figure 3-1 and see how justified text looks, remove align="justify" from the <P> paragraph tag so that the body text becomes flush left and looks more "relaxed."

Tip

Experiment with various alignments of the text.

Alignment of the elements within tables is a bit more complex; we cover that in Chapter 6, along with other information on tables. Likewise, image alignment, which we cover in Chapter 4, works a bit differently.

The BLOCKQUOTE element

The BLOCKQUOTE element can be particularly useful. Any text enclosed within a BLOCKQUOTE element is automatically indented from both sides of a Web page.

Here's how to use the BLOCKQUOTE element:

1. Enclose the text you want to make a block quote inside the `<BLOCKQUOTE>...</BLOCKQUOTE>` tags. On the Brown Family Links page, we enclose the quotation and the quotation's source, like so:

   ```
   <BLOCKQUOTE><P><I>With all beings and all
   things, we shall be as relatives.</I>
   <BR>—Sioux Indian saying</BLOCKQUOTE>
   ```

2. Save the file.

3. Display the Web page in your browser. Figure 3-2 shows the results.

As you can see the BLOCKQUOTE text is set off from the other text on the page.

The CENTER element

The CENTER element is one of the simplest and most useful of all HTML elements. It solves a number of problems. By enclosing text or images on a Web page within the `<CENTER>...</CENTER>` tags, you can center one or more elements simultaneously.

Figure 3-2: Indent text on both the left and right sides with the BLOCKQUOTE element.

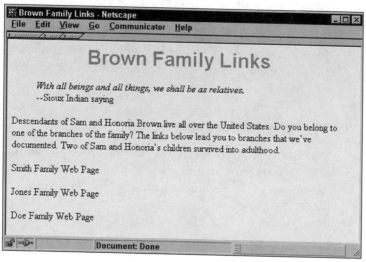

To see how the CENTER element works, replace the `<BLOCKQUOTE>...</BLOCKQUOTE>` tags that you added in the previous section with the `<CENTER>...</CENTER>` tags. The code should look like this:

```
<CENTER><P><I>With all beings and all things, we
shall be as relatives.</I>
<BR>—Sioux Indian saying
</CENTER>
```

Figure 3-3 shows the result.

Dividing Up Pages with Rules

The HR (horizontal rule) element is a simple and intuitive part of HTML. At its most basic, the HR element is nothing more than a straight line that's drawn across the page to separate two sections from each other, just the way you use a stroke of a pen to do the same thing on a piece of paper.

Figure 3-3: Centering Web page elements.

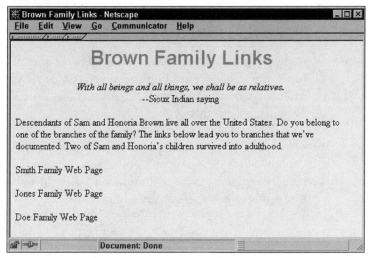

Horizontal rules have only four attributes — `align`, `noshade`, `size`, and `width`. The `size` attribute really should be called "height" because that's what it sets, but you can't have everything.

Internet Explorer also accepts a `color` attribute for the HR element, but Netscape Navigator does not recognize it.

Here's the lowdown on each attribute:

- The `align` attribute takes a value of left, center, or right. The default value is center.

- The `size` attribute takes a value of the number of pixels in the line's height. This attribute has no official default value but is generally between 4 to 6 pixels high in most browsers, if you don't specify a size.

- The `width` attribute takes a value either in pixels or in percentage of the screen's width. The default value is 100 percent of the width of the screen.

■ The noshade attribute is unique to the HR element. A horizontal rule, by default, is hollow. In the old days of medium gray backgrounds, this characteristic made the rule look as though it were embedded in the Web page, or shaded, although the effect is not so apparent on other background colors. Adding the noshade attribute makes a solid line. No value is assigned to the noshade attribute; it's just there or not there.

Although by default the <HR> tag inserts a horizontal rule that extends across the entire width of a Web page, you can choose whatever percentage you want. Here's how to add a horizontal rule to a Web page:

1. Place the tag <HR width="xx%"> wherever you want the rule to appear. (The xx represents whatever percentage you choose.) For the example, put <HR> tags above and below the quotation, setting the width value of each to 50%. Here's the code:

```
<CENTER>
<HR width="50%">
<P><I>With all beings and all things, we shall
be as relatives.</I>
<BR>—Sioux Indian saying
<HR width="50%">
<BR>
</CENTER>
```

2. Save the file.

3. Display the Web page in your browser. Figure 3-4 shows the results.

Figure 3-4:   Using the HR element.

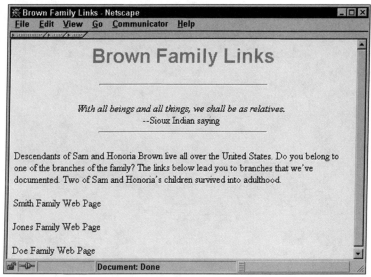

Notice that the quotation isn't centered vertically between the two horizontal rules. That's because the second line of the quotation ("Sioux Indian saying") uses the <BR> tag rather than the <P> tag. You can add an extra blank line by inserting <P> before the second horizontal rule, like this:

```
<CENTER>
<HR width="50%">
<P><I>With all beings and all things, we shall
be as relatives.</I>
<BR>—Sioux Indian saying
<P>
<HR width="50%">
</CENTER>
```

Figure 3-5 shows the result.

Figure 3-5: Use <P> to add an extra blank space on a Web page.

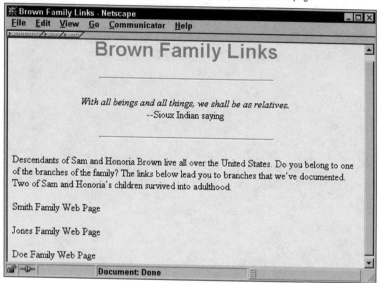

You may find it a bit odd that both the width attribute and the align attribute have default values set. The width is set to 100% by default, so you can't tell by looking at the horizontal rule that it has any alignment at all. Try it out — if the line extends all the way across the screen, setting the align attribute to left, center, or right doesn't matter. Only when the width is less than the screen width does the alignment matter at all.

Lots of people use graphic images of stylized lines instead of horizontal rules to divide page segments from one another. See Chapter 4 for information on inserting images.

Using Lists

The two main types of lists in HTML are technically known as *ordered* and *unordered lists*. Ordered lists are better known as *numbered lists*, and unordered lists are also called *bulleted lists*. This is because ordered lists use numbers (or letters) to notate items in the list, while unordered lists use bullets.

The fundamental difference between the two is implied in their names. You use ordered lists when the order of the list items is important, and you use unordered lists when the order isn't important. For example, if you want to create a list of steps, like the ones in this book, you use an ordered list because the steps have to be done sequentially. On the other hand, a list of programs that you own doesn't need to be in sequential order.

Both ordered lists (<OL>) and unordered lists (<UL>) use the same structure and have the LI (list item) element as their content. The LI element has an optional end tag, by the way, but it isn't really necessary. Browsers recognize that the beginning of the next list item means that the one before it has ended, and that the end of the list itself means that the last list item has ended.

Creating an unordered list

In unordered lists, you can determine how the actual bullet looks by setting the `type` attribute with one of the following values:

- `disc`: a solid circle (the default value)

- `circle`: a hollow circle

- `square`: a solid square

The square is supposed to be hollow, according to the HTML standard, but both major Web browsers show a solid square.

On the Brown Family Links page, the three paragraphs listing the Web pages of related families can make a perfect bulleted list. To create a bulleted list, follow these steps:

1. Enclose all the list items within the `<UL>`...`</UL>` tags. In the example, the code looks like this:

```
<UL>
<P>Smith Family Web Page
<P>Jones Family Web Page
<P>Doe Family Web Page
</UL>
```

2. Add `<LI>` tags before each list item. In the example, you also have to remove the `<P>` tags before each list item, like so:

```
<UL>
<LI>Smith Family Web Page
<LI>Jones Family Web Page
<LI>Doe Family Web Page
</UL>
```

3. Save the file.

4. Display the Web page in your browser. Figure 3-6 shows the result.

Figure 3-6: An unordered list.

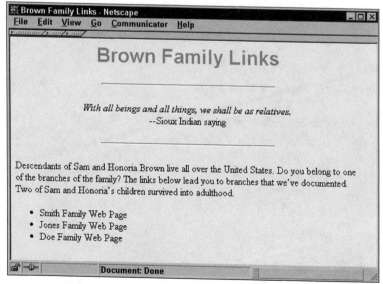

Creating an ordered list

For an ordered list, you can determine how the list is numbered by setting values for the `type` attribute. The value sets the numbering to Arabic numerals (the default setting), Roman numerals, or letters. Table 3-1 shows how the different values.

Table 3-1: **Values for the Ordered List Type Attribute**

Value	Result
1	Arabic numerals
I	Uppercase Roman numerals
i	Lowercase Roman numerals
A	Uppercase letters
a	Lowercase letters

Ordered lists have two more attributes that affect the numbering: `start` and `value`. By default, the first list item is numbered 1 (or A, a, and so on). The `start` attribute sets a different starting point for the list numbers. If you set it to a value of 5, for example, the first list item is numbered 5 instead of 1. If you're using Roman numerals, the first item is V (or v). If you're using letters, the first item is E (or e).

The `value` attribute works the same way, but you use it to set the number of an individual list item, rather than the list as a whole.

You create an ordered list just as you do an unordered list, except you use `<OL>...</OL>` tags instead of `<UL>...</UL>` tags.

CHAPTER 4
ADDING IMAGES

IN THIS CHAPTER

- Getting images
- Inserting images
- Aligning images
- Using background images

Images add immeasurably to the appearance of most Web pages. They break up what may otherwise be endless stretches of text. Properly chosen, images can increase your visitors' understanding of a topic or simply excite the artistic sense within us all. In this chapter, we get you started using images on your Web pages.

Images on the World Wide Web are usually in one of three file formats: GIF (Graphics Interchange Format), JPEG or JPG (Joint Photographic Experts Group), or PNG (Portable Network Graphics). These three formats work in any major Web browser. Other formats may or may not display properly, depending on the brand of browser. So you may want to play it safe and use one of the three common formats.

If you like a particular image that isn't in one of the usual formats, you can convert the format with an image processing program. You can also resize images to make the file size smaller. You can find these programs on the Web. Shareware programs, such as Paint Shop Pro (www.jasc.com) for Windows, may provide what you need.

Getting Images

You can get images from a number of sources on the Web. The images we use in this chapter were created with the sample Web site in mind. If you're replicating the example, you can download those images from the CliffsNotes Web site at `www.cliffsnotes.com`. Or you can substitute other images, if you prefer.

After you download the images from the CliffsNotes Web site, place the images in the same directory that contains the two Web pages you've already created.

The Resource Center lists a few Web sites from which you can download images.

Often, the artists who create the images allow only personal or private use of the images and prohibit their use on commercial Web sites. This means that you can use the images on your personal Web site as long as you aren't using your site to make money. Sometimes, the artist requests a small fee — in this case, you can download and try out the images for free, but if you keep them, you have to pay the fee to the artist. Be sure to read the fine print before you download images — and be kind to the artists by paying fees if applicable.

You can't just grab any image you want off the Web and use it on your own Web pages. You do have the ability to download it, but if someone else holds the copyright, you need permission to use it.

If you do decide to use someone else's image (and you get permission to do so), make sure that you download a copy of the image and upload that image to your own server, rather than use the other site as the image's source. Otherwise, that other Webmaster may get mad at you, because your users end up tying up his or her Web server resources every time they visit your page. Also, linking to a file on a site that you don't control isn't a good idea, because the other Webmaster may change the filename or location at some point.

Inserting Images

Not much in HTML is easier than inserting an image. At its most basic, all you do is add an IMG element to your source code and include its one absolutely required attribute — the src (source — location and name) of the image file.

The IMG element is an inline element, which means that you can, if you want to, place an image in the middle of a sentence. However, you may not often find a good, practical reason to do this, because most images are so much larger than the text that they simply disrupt the flow of the sentence.

Here's how to add an image to the Brown Family Home Page (adapt this procedure to add any image to any other Web page):

1. In your text editor, open the main.htm file that you worked on in Chapters 1 and 2.

2. Type the following code after the main heading for the page:

```
<IMG src="sam-honoria.jpg">
```

This tag tells the viewer's Web browser which image to insert there. If you haven't downloaded the sam-honoria.jpg image from the CliffsNotes Web site, go ahead and do so (or substitute an image of your own). Otherwise, your browser won't be able to display the image.

3. Save the file, keeping the name main.htm.

4. Display the Web page in your browser. Figure 4-1 shows the result.

Figure 4-1:   Inserting images.

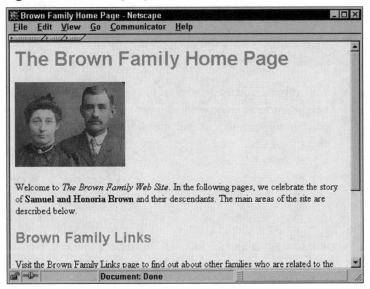

If the image isn't located in the same directory as the HTML file that accesses it, you need to include the path information as well as the file name in the `src` attribute. For now, keep everything simple by placing everything in the same directory. Also, `<IMG>` doesn't have an end tag.

Remember

Specifying width and height of an image

Though you don't have to, setting the `width` and `height` attributes for the image is a good idea. The value of these attributes is the number of pixels the image is wide and high. Although Web browsers can determine this, providing this information in advance does speed up page display a bit. You can get these values by loading the image into your Web browser the same way you do an HTML file (see Chapter 1) — the width and height show up in the title bar.

In the case of the Brown family photo you just added to your home page, if you know that the width is 184 pixels and the height is 136 pixels, you can speed up display for your viewers by adding that information to the IMG element, like this:

```
<IMG src="sam-honoria.jpg" width="184"
height="136">
```

The software you use to scan an image tells you its width and height. Alternatively, you can open an image in an image-editing program to find out the width and height. You can also set the width and height to values other than the correct values to stretch or compress the image. Changing the appearance of an image on the Web page in this way does not affect the actual image file in any way.

If you have an image that is too large to fit in the browser window or takes too long to download, you can use an image-editing program to decrease its size. Most programs enable you to proportionally decrease the width and height of an image, so that the image is not distorted and you don't have to guess what the proportional values would be. Just be sure that when you resize an image you save the altered image as a different file — that way, you don't alter the original image.

Setting borders

An image, by default, is borderless, which means that you don't see a box around it. Depending on the particular graphic, adding a border may add to or detract from its appearance. If an image doesn't have a border, it may appear to "float" on the page, which may or may not be your intention.

The `border` attribute takes a numerical value that sets the thickness of the border in pixels. Here's how to add a border to an image:

1. In the IMG element, add the attribute `border="x"`. In the example, we defined the x value of the border as 2.

```
<IMG src="sam-honoria.jpg" width="184"
height="136" border="2">
```

2. Save the file.

3. Display the Web page in your browser. Figure 4-2 shows
   the result.

Figure 4-2:   Adding a border to an image.

Using alternative text

At times, having an alternative display for an image is important. The file may be unavailable (perhaps moved to a new
location and the src attribute not updated). Perhaps it's
merely a large file that's slow in downloading, and you want
to give your users a clue to what's coming in. A number of
programs used to access the Web aren't visual browsers, such
as the speech synthesizers used by people who are blind. And
then there are those people who turn off images to speed up
their Web access.

In any of these cases, the alt attribute comes into play. It
enables you to add alternative text that appears in place of

the image. The value of the attribute is simply the text that you want to display, as in the following code:

```
<IMG src="sam-honoria.jpg" width="184"
height="136" border="2" alt="Portrait of Sam and
Honoria Brown">
```

Figure 4-3 shows the alternative text in action when your cursor hovers over a missing figure.

Figure 4-3:   Alternative text tells viewers what they're missing if they can't view an image.

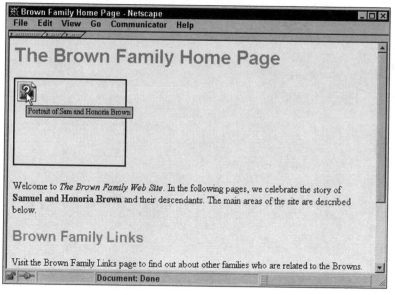

Using images with transparent backgrounds

An image with a transparent background is a kind of GIF image that doesn't appear to have a visible background. The image seems to float over the background of the Web page. In order to create such an image, you need to work with an image-editing program, such as Paint Shop Pro (`www.jasc.com`).

Creating such an image yourself doesn't pertain to HTML and is therefore beyond the scope of this book. However, adding a transparent image is the same as adding a regular image. Here we add an *inline image* (or an image inserted into a line of text) to the Family Links Page:

1. Open the Brown Family Links page (links.htm) in your text editor.

2. Position the text cursor where you want the image to appear. In the example, place the cursor between <LI> and the word *Doe*.

3. Enter the IMG element, like so:

    ```
    <LI><IMG src="New.gif">Doe Family Web Page
    ```

    This code tells the browser which image to insert. If you haven't downloaded the New.gif image from the Cliffs-Notes Web site, please do so. Otherwise, your browser won't be able to display the image.

4. Save your changes and open the file in your Web browser. As shown in Figure 4-4, the image appears to be floating next to the Doe Family Web Page list item.

Figure 4-4: An inline image added to a line of text.

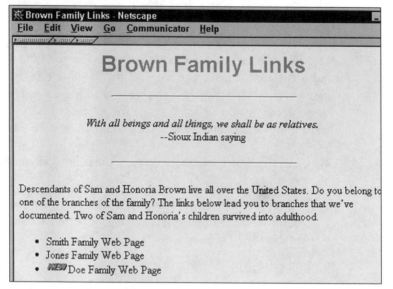

Aligning Images

Image alignment is a tricky thing. You have five official values for the IMG element's `align` attribute: bottom, middle, top, left, and right. The first three don't actually have anything to do with aligning the image. Instead, they align the baseline of the text (or other element) that's next to the image with the image itself. (Bottom is the default.)

The `align="left"` and `align="right"` settings are where it gets really strange, though. If you use them, the image moves away from where it was originally placed and lands against either the left or right margin. This is called *floating* the image. The text then wraps around it.

For some bizarre reason, center is not an option for the `align` attribute. However, you can center an image on a Web page by placing it within a CENTER element.

Here is how to change the right or left alignment of an image, using the Brown Family Home Page as an example:

1. Open the main.htm file in your text editor.

2. Add the `align="right"` attribute to the IMG element, like this:

```
<IMG src="sam-honoria.jpg" width="184"
height="136" border="2" alt="Portrait of Sam
and Honoria Brown" align="right">
```

3. Save the file.

4. Display the page in your Web browser. The effect is shown in Figure 4-5.

Figure 4-5:   Right-aligning an image.

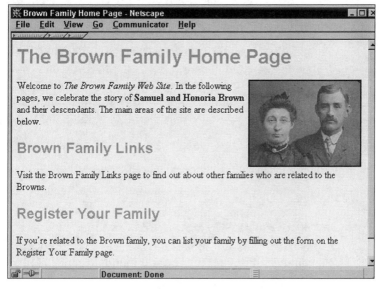

As you can see, the image shifted over to the right margin and the text wrapped around it.

Using Background Images

A background image works a little bit differently from a normal image. You don't use the IMG element at all. Instead, you use an attribute of the BODY element — the background attribute. And because it's an attribute and not an element, it has no attributes of its own, only the value, which is the location of the image file.

The background attribute is similar to the background color (bgcolor) attribute in Chapter 2, except you define an image as the value instead of a color.

A background attribute also behaves differently. While a normal image just lands wherever you put it and stays there, a background image tiles (or repeats itself) across and down the page until it fills the entire Web page.

Everything else on the page (text, images, and so on) sits on top of the background image. Because of this, you may want to choose a background image that's not too busy or a pattern that doesn't clash with the foreground material. Many Web designers make sure that their backgrounds are faded for this reason.

To set a background image, follow these steps:

1. Open the links.htm file in your text editor.

2. Place the background attribute and its value in the <BODY> tag. In this example, we add a faded image of an old sailing ship to the background, like so:

```
<BODY bgcolor="beige" background="ship.gif">
```

The background attribute, just like the src attribute in the IMG element, tells the browser which image to place. If you haven't yet downloaded the ship.gif from the CliffsNotes Web site, go ahead and do so. Otherwise, your browser won't be able to display the image.

3. Save the file.

4. Display the Web page in your browser. Figure 4-6 shows the result.

Figure 4-6:   A background image.

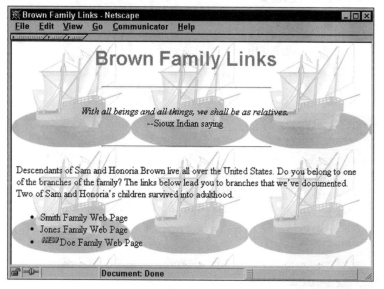

As you can see, the background image jazzes up the visual aspect of the page quite a bit, while not interfering with the readability of the text.

Images add a new dimension to Web pages. Another thing that makes Web pages unique is the fact that you can link text and images to other Web pages, as you see in the next chapter.

CHAPTER 5

WORKING WITH LINKS

IN THIS CHAPTER

- Understanding URLs
- Creating links
- Assigning colors to links
- Using named anchors
- Creating e-mail links

Links, above all else, are what make the World Wide Web an exciting, interconnected network. Without links, you'd have only a bunch of totally separate pages of structured text. However, the ability to link those separate files together has created something unprecedented in human history. With every Web page on the Net accessible by some route from every other Web page, the World Wide Web is the largest single document ever created.

Understanding URLs

If you want to send a messenger to pick up a document, you tell him what address to go to and the name of the document. And that's exactly how the World Wide Web works. Your Web browser sends a request for a file that has a particular address on a *Web server* (the computer that holds the HTML file), and the Web server sends a copy of that file to your browser.

Addresses on the Internet are called *Uniform Resource Locators* (*URLs*, for short). For example, a URL, such as `http://www.idgbooks.com/books/cliffsnotes/` `webpages.htm`, has the following four parts:

■ The protocol, or method by which your computer communicates with the remote one. (It's always `http://` for a Web server.)

■ The server address — in this case, `www.idgbooks.com`.

■ The path to the directory on the server where the file is located — in this case, `/books/cliffsnotes/`.

■ The name of the file — in this example, `webpages.htm`.

The third part (the path) is often unused because many (if not most) Web pages are kept in the HTML root directory of the Web server. For example, the following URL, using the protocol, the server address, and the name of the HTML file, takes you to the IDG Books Worldwide home page:

    http://www.idgbooks.com/index.htm

Because the standard filename index.htm is used by most Web servers as the default page when no other page is specified, the following URL also takes you to the IDG Books Worldwide home page:

    http://www.idgbooks.com

This type of URL is known as an *absolute URL*. An absolute URL specifies all the information needed to find any file on the Internet from anywhere else on the Net. But what if you want to make a link from one Web page to another page on the same site? You can still use an absolute URL, but you don't really need to.

In that case, you can use a shortened form called a *relative URL*. If the file is in the same directory as the one holding the Web page that has the link, all you need to use is the name of the file you want to link to. For example, say that you want to create a link from your home page that's located at `http://www.myserver.com/index.html` to a page in the same directory called `myresume.html`. The absolute URL to it would be `http://www.myserver.com/myresume.html`, but all you really need to say is `myresume.html`. The Web browser understands that it's a local file. If it's in another directory on the same server, you need to include the path to that directory as well as the name of the file. For example, if the HTML file is in a different directory called `business`, you'd use `business/myresume.html` as the relative URL.

Creating Links

Although URLs are used in a variety of HTML elements, the most common is the A (anchor) element, which uses a start tag and end tag: `<A>...</A>`. Links are a two-way phenomenon. The anchor on your Web page is one end of the link, and the Web page you're linking to is the other end. The A element that you create is known as the *source anchor* and the other Web page is called the *destination anchor*. Web browsers can move back and forth along this link (which is exactly what their Back and Forward buttons do).

Text and image links

The two key parts of the A element are the content and the URL of the destination anchor, which is specified with the `href` (hypertext reference) attribute. The content — the part between the start tag `<A href>` and the end tag `</A>` — is the only part of the element that's visible on the Web page, and it can be either text or an image. Because the A element is inline, you can embed links in the midst of other material.

For example, one word in a sentence can have its own link without involving any of the surrounding text.

The Brown Family Links page in this book's running example has a bulleted list, each item of which needs to be linked to a different URL. You can create these links by using the A element with an absolute URL.

All the URLs and family names used in this chapter, and in this book's example pages, are fictitious.

Using the running example to illustrate, these steps show you how to create links from your Web page to external Web sites:

1. Open the file links.htm in your text editor.

2. Enclose the first item in the bulleted list, "Smith Family Web Page," in <A href>...</A> tags to link it to the URL http://www.smithfamilypg.com, like so:

```
<LI>
<A href="http://www.smithfamilypg.com">Smith
Family Web Page</A>
```

3. Link the second item in the bulleted list to the URL http://www.jonesfamilypg.com:

```
<LI>
<A href="http://www.jonesfamilypg.com">Jones
Family Web Page</A>
```

4. Link the third item in the bulleted list to the URL http://www.doefamilypg.com:

```
<LI><IMG src="New.gif">
<A href="http://www.doefamilypg.com">Doe
Family Web Page</A>
```

5. Save the file.

6. Display the Web page in your browser. When you pass the mouse pointer over the link, you see the destination appear in the browser's status bar (at the bottom of the screen), as shown in Figure 5-1.

Figure 5-1: Adding links to other Web sites.

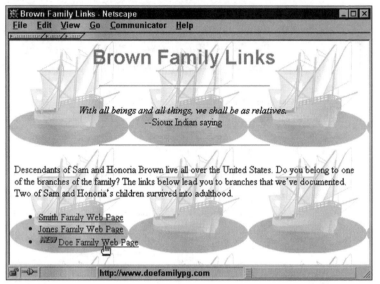

You can copy URLs and paste them into HTML documents. That way, you don't have to type them from scratch and risk introducing errors. Just display in your browser the Web page you want to link to, highlight the URL in the address bar, and copy.

Don't forget to test all your links before you post your page on the Web. However, if you test the links you added in this section, you receive an error message in your browser because the links are fictitious. If you want to use a real URL, simply copy and paste one from your browser's address bar into the code, save the document, and then test the link in your browser.

Linking to other pages on your site

Though you can use absolute links to link pages within a single site, you may find that using relative links is much easier, because all you have to do is specify the path to the destination file.

To demonstrate how to create relative links, we use the Brown Family Home Page (main.htm) to link to the Brown Family Links page (links.htm) and to a third page that you haven't created yet (register.htm). To keep things simple, you should have all these files in the same directory. Keep in mind that you can use these techniques for any Web site you create.

Tip

When creating links within a single site, planning what you want to do ahead of time is always a good idea. You may even want to sketch on a piece of paper all the documents you want to create for a site and how you want to link them. For this book's running example, we knew we wanted to create a Web site that had three pages, and we decided that the main page would link to the other two. Such planning ahead can make your Web site-designing life much easier.

Using the running example to illustrate, these steps show you how to create links from your Web page to other pages in your Web site:

1. Open the file main.htm in your text editor.

2. Scroll to the paragraph that begins "Visit the Brown Family Links page . . ." and enclose the phrase *Brown Family Links* in <A href>...</A> tags, like so:

```
<P>Visit the <A href="links.htm">Brown Family
Links</A> page to find out about other
families who are related to the Browns.
```

Notice that all you have to use as the `href` value is the name of the links.htm file. Much simpler than including the entire absolute URL. Relative links also load faster in visitors' browsers — your visitors appreciate that.

3. In the paragraph that begins "If you're related to . . .," enclose the phrase *Register Your Family* in `<A href>...</A>` tags, like so:

```
<P>If you're related to the Brown family, you
can list your family by filling out the form
on the <A href="register.htm">Register Your
Family</A> page.
```

Because you just created a link to a nonexistent page, you may want to go ahead and create an empty document so that you don't forget to do it later. Don't worry, you get to use that document in Chapter 7. But for now, just use your text editor's New command to create a new document, and then save that document with the name register.htm in the directory that holds the other HTML documents for the Web site.

4. Save your changes to the main.htm document.

5. Load the page in your Web browser. You can see the two underlined hyperlinks in Figure 5-2.

Be sure to test the links before you post any page on the Web. In the example, when you click the <u>Brown Family Links</u> link, the links page (links.htm) appears in your browser. When you click the <u>Register Your Family</u> link, the blank document you created (register.htm) appears. To return to the Brown Family Home Page from either page, just click the Back button of your browser.

Figure 5-2:   Linking from one page on your site to another.

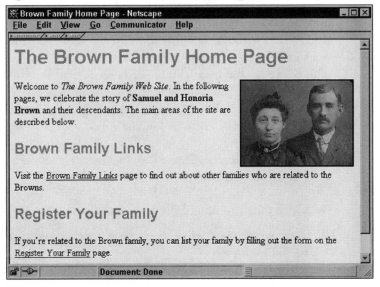

Changing the link colors

If you don't like having blue links, you can reset them at will. However, you can't set the color of an individual link. This is a global setting affecting the color of all the links. The link colors are found in three attributes of the BODY element. The `link` attribute sets the color of unvisited links, `vlink` sets the color of visited links, and `alink` sets the color of a link during the instant that it's being clicked.

The following code demonstrates how to set link colors:

```
<BODY link="red" vlink="white" alink="cyan">
```

Most people are very used to the normal link colors. Change them only if you have to. For example, change the link color to make it show up better against a particular background color.

Creating E-mail Links

You can add your own e-mail address as a link on your Web page. When visitors click that link, their e-mail programs open and display an empty e-mail form that's preaddressed with your e-mail address. Visitors need only to type in a message and click the Send button to send you the message. Creating an e-mail link (often called a `mailto` link) is virtually identical to creating any other kind of link.

Using the Brown Family Home Page to illustrate, these steps show you how to create an e-mail link on a Web page:

1. Open the main.htm file in your text editor.

2. Place your cursor before the copyright notice and type the following text:

```
<P>Contact Us
```

3. Enclose the words *Contact Us* in `<A>...</A>` tags and add the attribute `href="mailto:webmaster@ brownfoundation.com"`, like so:

```
<P><A
href="mailto:webmaster@brownfoundation.com">Co
ntact Us</A>
```

4. Save your changes.

5. Open the main.htm page in your Web browser to view the new link, as shown in Figure 5-3.

Figure 5-3: A `mailto` hyperlink to an e-mail address.

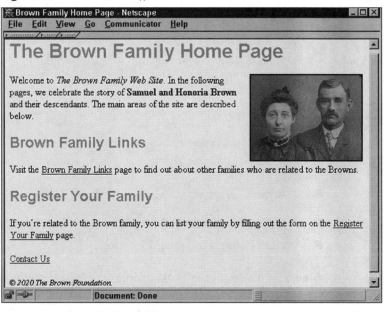

The above e-mail address is fictitious. If you click the link, your e-mail program still opens and preaddresses a message box, but if you send the message, it will probably be returned to you as undeliverable.

Try putting your own e-mail address in the code. You should be able to send yourself a message to make sure that the link works!

CHAPTER 6

CREATING AND USING TABLES

IN THIS CHAPTER

- Making a basic table
- Setting cell height and width
- Using cell alignment
- Setting cell padding and spacing
- Understanding word wrap

A table is a versatile HTML feature that enables you to arrange contents in rows and columns. You can use tables in a straightforward way to present data, similar to using a spreadsheet, or you can use them to jazz up the layout of an existing Web page. In this chapter, you learn the basics of working with tables.

If you're following along with this book's running example, you need to download a few images from the CliffsNotes Web site at www.cliffsnotes.com. So go ahead and download these files: Crest1.gif, Crest2.gif, and Crest3.gif. And don't forget to save them in the same directory as your other Web site files.

Remember in Chapter 1 that we recommend that you preview your Web pages in both major browsers because each browser handles HTML a little differently. Tables are a prime example of how the browsers differ. We use Navigator throughout this chapter, but be aware that your results may vary a bit if you use Internet Explorer.

Anatomy of a Basic Table

In Figure 6-1, you see the framework of a Web page table, and what each part is called.

Figure 6-1:   The parts of a simple Web page table.

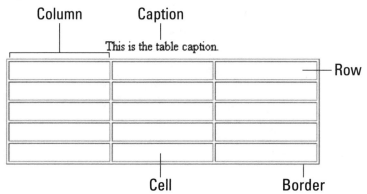

In HTML, you create tables (not surprisingly) with the TABLE element. Contained within that element are TR (table row) elements and an optional CAPTION element, which you can use to name the table. The TR elements in turn contain TD (table data) elements, which hold the actual visible content. Here is what the code (with no content) looks like for the table in Figure 6-1; the nonbreaking spaces ( ) allow the cells to appear empty. You can easily see how the table is structured.

```
<TABLE>
<CAPTION align="top">Caption</CAPTION>
<TR>
 <TD> </TD>
 <TD> </TD>
 <TD> </TD>
</TR>
<TR>
 <TD> </TD>
 <TD> </TD>
```

```
 <TD> </TD>
</TR>
<TR>
 <TD> </TD>
 <TD> </TD>
 <TD> </TD>
</TR>
<TR>
 <TD> </TD>
 <TD> </TD>
 <TD> </TD>
</TR>
<TR>
 <TD> </TD>
 <TD> </TD>
 <TD> </TD>
</TR>
</TABLE>
```

A variation on the basic TD element is called the TH (table header) element, which you can use to create headings for each column of the table. The content of the TH element is centered and boldface by default. If you don't want this look, just use a regular TD element and modify the alignment and font characteristics of the cell's contents to suit your needs.

Each cell in a table is basically a miniature Web page of its own, which means that if you can put an element on a Web page, you can put it into a table cell. A cell can have its own background color, background image, links, text, images, and even other tables. And you can modify the contents of table cells exactly as you modify the contents of a plain Web page.

The TR, TD, and TH elements don't require end tags, although you can supply them if you wish.

Here are a few other things to remember when working with tables:

- Just as you set the HR element, you can set the alignment of a table to left, center, or right and specify the table's width as a certain number of pixels or a percentage of the Web page's width.

- You can align the CAPTION element to the top or bottom of the table, which means that the caption is centered above or below the table. You can also set the caption alignment to left or right, although those settings don't do precisely what they imply and currently they only work in Internet Explorer. The settings actually align the caption to the top left or top right, not the left or right sides, of the table.

- Like the IMG element, tables have an optional border. You can set the border size anywhere from 0 (invisible) on up.

Make sure that each row has the same number of cells. Otherwise, your table looks ragged.

Creating a Table on a Web Page

To add a table to a Web page, you use the `<TABLE>...</TABLE>` tags, which enclose all the other tags that define rows, columns, captions, and so on. You can use tables to modify the layout of any Web page. Here we show you how to do just that to the Brown Family Links page.

In Chapter 5, you added a bulleted list of links to the Brown Family Links page — which looks fine, if a little boring. But with a table, you can enhance the layout and even add images that line up neatly with the text. Using the links page to illustrate, the following steps show you how to use a table to enhance the look of a Web page:

1. Open the links.htm file in your text editor.

2. Scroll down to the bulleted list, as designated by the `<UL>`, `<LI>`, and `</UL>` tags. Delete these tags so that you can convert the list to a table. (Be careful not to delete the `<A href>` link tags — you want to preserve the links.)

3. Position your cursor right before the text that you want to make into a table. In the example, that's before "Smith Family Web Page." Type in the following code to begin the table:

```
<TABLE border="5" bgcolor="#FFFFFF"
bordercolor="000066" cellspacing="0">
```

This code specifies the table border as 5 pixels wide and the cell spacing as 0 (for more on cell spacing, see "Setting Cell Padding and Spacing" later in this chapter). The code also sets the color of the table's entire background and assigns a color to the border (see Chapter 2 for more on adding color to Web page elements).

Tip

You may be wondering why the `cellspacing` attribute is included if its value is set to 0. The default value for this attribute is actually 2 pixels, which allows the background image to show through the border in Navigator. (In Internet Explorer, the borders are opaque.) By specifying the attribute to 0, you eliminate the bleed-through; the borders appear as solid lines.

4. To give your table a name, use the CAPTION element, like so:

```
<CAPTION align="top"><B>Related
Families</B></CAPTION>
```

We decided to call the table "Related Families" and to top-align the caption, which means that it's centered above the rest of the table.

5. Begin adding your table rows by using the TR element.
In this example, we added a table header (TH) for each
column. Remember, the TH element must go within a
TR element, like this:

```
<TR>
<TH>Family Crest</TH>

<TH>About This Family</TH>
</TR>
```

This code creates two table headers in the same table row,
which means that the table will have two columns —
with a header for each.

6. Add more table rows as you need them. If you're replicating the book's example, add the images (which you downloaded earlier) for the related families' crests in the first
column and move the links to the second column. Use the
TD (table data) element to define the content of each cell.
Here's what the code for the remaining rows looks like:

```
<TR>
<TD width="20%"><IMG src="Crest1.gif"
border="0" height="88" width="60"></TD>

<TD>
<A href="http://www.smithfamilypg.com">Smith
Family Web Page.</A>Augustus Smith married
Euphonia Brown in 1921. The Smiths are located
in 12 countries around the world.</TD>
</TR>
```

The preceding code specifies that the first row in the
body of the table contains two table cells, each of which
is marked with TD. The first cell contains the image
named Crest1.gif, which is 88 pixels high and 60 pixels
wide and does not have a visible border. The second cell
in the row contains the hyperlinked phrase <u>Smith Family Web Page</u>, which when clicked, takes you to the

mythical URL `http://www.smithfamilypg.com`. This link is followed by two descriptive sentences about the Smith family.

```
<TR>
<TD width="20%"><IMG src="Crest2.gif"
border="0" height="88" width="60"></TD>

<TD>
<A href="http://www.jonesfamilypg.com">Jones
Family Web Page.</A>Marmaduke Jones married
Anastasia Brown in 1919. The Browns have 1,033
relations around the United States!</TD>
</TR>
```

This row is structured the same as the preceding one, except that the image source file and the hyperlink are different.

```
<TR>
<TD width="20%"><IMG src="Crest3.gif"
BORDER="0" height="88" width="60"></TD>

<TD width="20%"><IMG src="NEW.GIF" height="17"
width="33">
<A href="http://www.doefamilypg.com">Doe
Family Web Page.</A>The Doe Family is a new
addition to the Web site—if you're related,
you can add your name by filling out this
site's registration form.</TD>
</TR>
```

This row is structured the same as the preceding two, except that the second cell contains an image file named `new.gif` that is 17 pixels high and 33 pixels wide. The image source for the family crest and the hyperlink also differ.

Whew! That's a lot of code to wade through. Figure 6-2 shows the result of your hard work.

Figure 6-2:   Your new table.

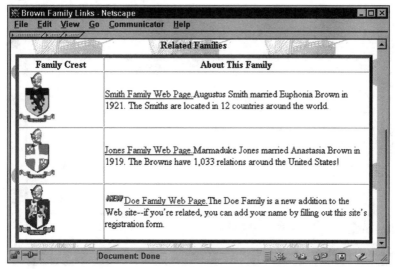

You may notice in Figure 6-2 that not much space exists between the links (such as <u>Smith Family Web Page</u>) and the following text. You can add more space by inserting nonbreaking spaces ( ). Figure 6-3 shows what happens when you add one nonbreaking space after each link.

The TABLE and CAPTION elements require end tags, and the CAPTION element must come first after the <TABLE> start tag.

Setting Cell Height or Width

You can set the height or width of any cell independently of all the other cells. Just as you can with the table itself, you can set this value either to a specific value in pixels or to a percentage value. However, the percentage in this case is a percentage of the table's width or height, not of the Web page.

Make sure that the percentages of all cells combined in a particular row or column add up to 100.

Figure 6-3: Adding spaces to separate words on a Web page.

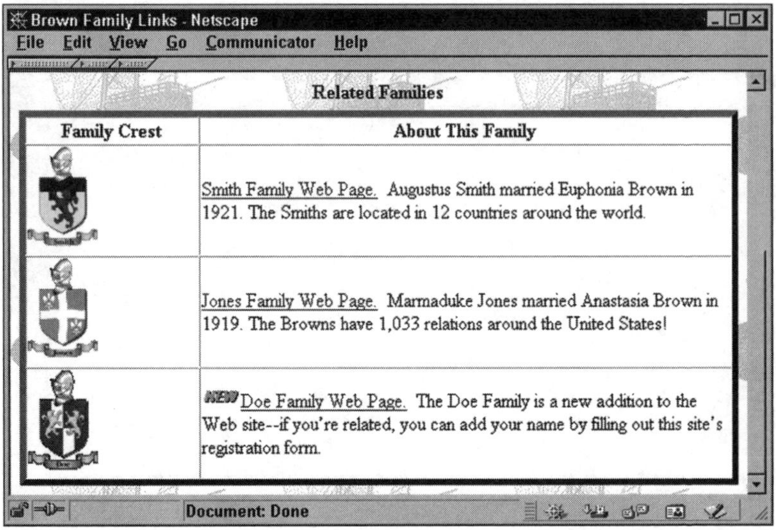

Because a table is composed of rows and columns of data, the value you set for one cell automatically affects related cells. For example, all the cells in one row are the height of the highest cell in that row. Likewise, all the cells in one column are the same width.

Try playing with the cell dimensions of the table you created in the previous section. In the running example (refer to Figure 6-3), you can see that the first column of cells is wider than it needs to be. The first cell in the first column is set to be 20 percent of the width of the entire table (`<TD width="20%">`). By changing the width to 10 percent, you can make all the cells in the column slightly smaller. Here's what the resulting code looks like:

```
<TD width="10%"><IMG src="Crest2.gif" border="0"
height="88" width="60"></TD>
```

Changing the width of the first column provides more room for the table's second column, which now occupies the remaining 90 percent of the table's width, instead of 80 percent. Figure 6-4 shows the result.

Figure 6-4:   Tweaking the column width of a table.

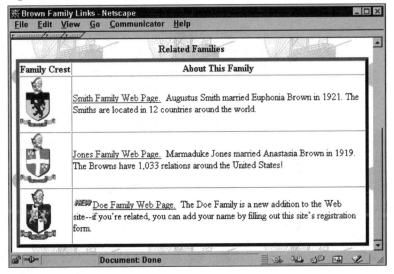

If you want the table cell to automatically set itself to the size of an image, do not include `width` or `height` attributes for the cell.

Tables don't always do exactly what you tell them to do. Sometimes, you can't make a cell too small because the text or image within the cell is larger than the size you specify. In cases like that, the Web browser makes the width of the cell slightly larger than the width of the text or the image that the cell contains.

Using Cell Alignment

Cell alignment is a matter of inheritance, which means that if you don't specify the alignment for a particular cell, the alignment of its contents is determined by the alignment value of its parent element. For example, if you set an alignment value for the TR element, that value applies to all the TD elements within it, unless you override it by setting a specific value for a TD element.

The `align` attribute deals with horizontal alignment and has possible values of left, center, or right. The `valign` attribute takes care of vertical alignment and has values of top, middle, or bottom. The default horizontal alignment for cell content is left and the default vertical alignment is bottom.

To modify the cell alignment in a cell, simply add the `align` and `valign` attributes and their appropriate values. In the running example, we made each of the crest images centered both horizontally and vertically. Just add the following attributes to the TD element for each crest image:

```
align="center" valign="middle"
```

The code for the first crest image should look like this:

```
<TD align="center" valign="middle"><IMG
src="Crest1.gif" border="0" height="88"
width="60"></TD>
```

The code for the other crest images should be formatted similarly. Figure 6-5 shows the result.

Figure 6-5:   Adjusting the alignment of cell content.

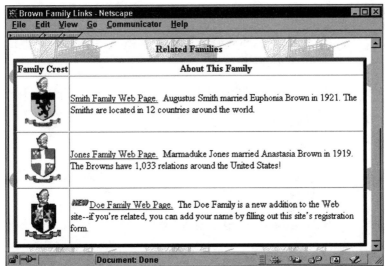

Setting Cell Padding and Spacing

Cell padding sets a bit of room between the walls of a cell and the contents of that cell. *Cell spacing* does much the same thing on the outside of the cell; it puts room between the cells themselves, as well as between the cells and the border.

While cell spacing must be a value in pixels, cell padding can be a percentage or a pixel value. So, if cell padding is a pixel value, the contents of the cell are exactly that far away from the cell walls. If the cell padding is a percentage value, the cell contents are half of that value away from the cell walls; this situation occurs because the percentage is divided in two and applied to the top and bottom and the left and right sides. For example, if the cell padding is set to 20 percent, the actual distance is 10 percent on each side.

Tip

Depending on how you're using the table, you may or may not want to change these settings. Text generally looks better with some cell padding — otherwise, the text tends to run into the cell walls. But images often look better with no space around them.

To add cell padding and spacing to any table, simply add the cellpadding and cellspacing attributes and their values to the TABLE element. Here's how we modified the Family Links table:

```
<TABLE border="5" cellspacing="6" cellpadding="6"
bgcolor="#FFFFFF" bordercolor="000066">
```

Figure 6-6 shows the result.

Figure 6-6: Adjusting cell padding and spacing.

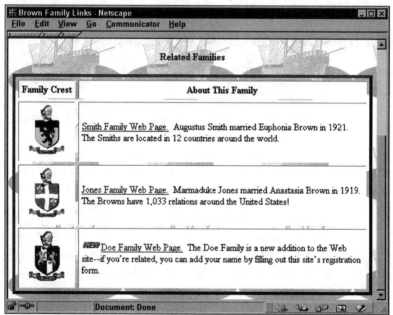

You may notice in Navigator that the background image shows through the cell borders. In Internet Explorer, those cell borders appear opaque, and you can even assign to them a color other than white. Navigator currently offers you no way to make the borders appear opaque or in a different color — perhaps later versions will incorporate this feature. For now, if you don't like the bleed-through you see in Navigator (and we don't), you may want to set the `cellspacing` attribute back to 0, so that the cell borders appear as solid lines in both browsers. Doing so won't affect the `cellpadding` attribute at all.

Try different values to see what looks best for your needs.

Understanding Word Wrap

Text normally wraps around when it reaches the wall of a cell, beginning another line as necessary. However, you can set the `nowrap` attribute in a cell. This setting causes the cell width to continue expanding to hold the text rather than the text accommodating the cell size. Even if the width of that cell is specifically set, that setting is automatically overridden. You won't see many practical applications for this function, but you may want to use it, for example, when formatting a poem, where the lines shouldn't be broken.

If you use the `nowrap` attribute, the text may expand horizontally beyond the width of the browser window, requiring your visitors to scroll horizontally to see all of the text. Consider carefully before using the `nowrap` attribute.

If you use the `nowrap` attribute, you can still force line breaks by using the P and BR elements.

Making Borders Invisible

Often, the most effective Web page tables have borders that are invisible — that is, the cell borders and/or the outside table border are set to "0." By making borders invisible, you can align the text or images that are contained in the table cells, but the table border doesn't interfere with the text. That way, the reader can concentrate on the contents, not on the table structure.

The code for an invisible border attribute looks like this:

```
<TABLE border="0">
```

You can still adjust cell padding and spacing attributes to alter the spacing between columns and rows. But keep in mind that because you've made the borders invisible, the dividing lines between the cells won't be visible.

Figure 6-7 shows what would happen if you made the borders of the Related Families table invisible. In our opinion, this doesn't look very good design-wise. We would opt to retain the borders in this case — but you may think differently for the tables on your own Web page.

Figure 6-7:   Making table borders invisible.

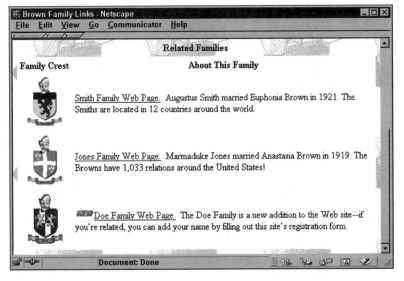

CHAPTER 7

USING FORMS

IN THIS CHAPTER

- Understanding how forms work
- Understanding the INPUT element
- Adding a TEXTAREA element
- Creating a drop-down menu with SELECT and OPTION

Forms enable you to gather data from the people who visit your site. In HTML, you can use a variety of data-entry elements to allow users to enter data directly or choose among various options. Several types of data-entry elements exist, ranging from simple boxes for text entry to more complex drop-down lists of options. Users input data into these elements and then submit the data to the Web server that hosts your Web site. A special program, called a *CGI script*, processes that data and presents the data to you in a form that you can read and use.

Forms can be a complicated business. In fact, the intricacies of forms could take up an entire book in itself. So if you're really serious about using forms, you may want to investigate other resources that go into forms in more detail. In this chapter, we show you how to create the front end of the forms process — a simple form that your users can fill out and submit. However, creating the back end — the CGI script that processes the data — is beyond the scope of this book. The good news is that you can download tons of scripts that are already written; all you have to do is adapt them for your purposes.

Designing Your Forms

Most forms are carefully structured. When designing your forms, you need to make sure that you accommodate every possible contingency. For example, a text box with space for no more than seven characters doesn't make sense as a place for visitors to enter a city name. A box for entering zip codes must take into account that some people use five digits, while others use nine.

All the data-entry elements within a form require a `name` attribute. This attribute enables the results of the form to be determined — each name matches up with whatever information is entered or selected in the appropriate field. These matches are called *name/value pairs*. After the user completes the form, the name/value pairs are submitted at the click of a button.

What You Need to Use Forms

As mentioned previously, forms have two parts — the visible front end (the actual form that the user fills out) and the invisible back end (the CGI script).

A *CGI* (*Common Gateway Interface*) *script* is a computer program that processes the name/value pairs, and other data, and then saves the information for you to use. Such a script is written in a programming language, such as C++ or Perl. You don't really have to worry about what language the script is written in; all you need to know is whether your ISP can run a script written in that particular language. Before designing your forms, be sure to check with your ISP to make certain its Web server can run the script you want to use.

CGI programs handle form data for tasks such as the following:

- Managing guest books

- Updating simple databases

- Sending simultaneously an e-mail with a copy of the form's data to you and an e-mail thanking the person who filled out the form

The Resource Center at the end of this book points you toward a few places where you can download many CGI programs.

Creating a Web Page Form

The front end (or data-entry part) of a form is relatively easy to set up. After you identify a CGI program you want to use, you tell the form how to get that program. You do this with the action attribute in the FORM element's start tag, which has as its value the location and name of the program. Suppose that you're using a program called processthis.pl. (Perl programs end in the .pl file extension.) Your start tag may look like this:

```
<FORM action="/cgi-bin/processthis.pl"
method="post">
```

The cgi-bin/processthis.pl part of the code is the path to the CGI program. On most Web servers, CGI programs reside in the cgi-bin directory.

The method attribute, by the way, almost always has the value post. The only other option is the get method, which is rarely used. Post and get are two different ways of sending the information from the form to the CGI program.

Understanding the INPUT Element

The INPUT element can create most of the form features for collecting information from users. In fact, you can build a form that contains only INPUT elements. The reason is that this element is very flexible; its actual function and appearance depend on the value of its type attribute. This one element can give you a text box, a push button, or other controls in your form.

The INPUT element has no end tag.

Using text boxes

Text boxes enable your form's users to enter short segments of textual data, such as names and addresses. Two variations of the INPUT element do this — text and password. These two input types work exactly the same way, except that the password type substitutes asterisks for the characters the user enters. The asterisks provide a measure of security for users; for example, if a user types in a password to a bank account, someone looking over his or her shoulder can't see the actual password on-screen.

Whether you use the INPUT element to create a text box or a password box, you need to set the size attribute, which controls how wide the text box is. This attribute, however, does not limit the number of characters the box can contain — only how many characters can be seen on-screen at one time. If you set a text box to be 20 characters wide and then enter 30 characters into it, the text simply scrolls as you enter it. By default, the number of characters that can be entered is unlimited, but you can set the maxlength attribute to limit the number of characters. For example, if you set the maxlength attribute to 10, then no more than 10 characters can be entered regardless of how wide the text box is.

The value of a text box is the data that a user enters into it. However, you can set an initial value for the box via the `value` attribute. This initial value shows up on the form as its content and, unless the user changes it, is what is submitted. For instance, if you have a series of radio buttons, you can make one of them checked by default.

For this book's running example, you can create a form that enables relatives of the Brown family to submit information about themselves. Keep in mind that the guidelines in this chapter for creating forms can be applied to any Web page form you want to create.

The first step in constructing most forms is to set up some basic text-entry boxes with the tag `<INPUT type="text">`, followed by more specific size and value information. To add text boxes to the Register Your Family page, follow these steps:

1. Open the register.htm file in your text editor. Remember that you created the register.htm file back in Chapter 5.

2. Begin by setting up your document. In this example, we enter the HTML code that establishes this Web page and adds the colors and a heading that make it consistent with the other two Web pages on the site. We also add some introductory text for the form. Here's what the code looks like:

```
<HTML>

<HEAD>
<TITLE>Register Your Family</TITLE>
</HEAD>

<BODY bgcolor="beige">
```

```
<H1 align="center"><FONT color="rosybrown"
face="Arial, Helvetica, sans-serif">Register
Your Family</FONT></H1>

<P>Are you related to the Brown family? If so,
your family can be included on this Web site.
Fill out the form below and click Submit to
send us the information. We'll gladly add your
family to the <A href="links.htm"> Brown
Family Links</A> page.

</BODY>

</HTML>
```

3. Add a few blank lines before the </BODY> tag and type
in the two parts of the FORM element before </BODY>:

```
<FORM method="post" action="/cgi-
bin/mailform.pl">
</FORM>
```

The `cgi-bin/mailform.pl` is the location of the
CGI program that processes the data from the form.

4. Between these two tags, which enclose the visible data-
entry parts of the form, enter text instructions that define
text boxes, plus textual labels that tell users what information is required. Here's what the code for the example looks like:

```
<FORM method="post" action="/cgi-
bin/mailform.pl">

<P><B>Your name:</B>

<INPUT type="text" size="20" name="username">

<P><B>Your e-mail address:</B>

<INPUT type="text" size="20" name="address">
```

```
<P><B>Web site URL (if applicable):</B>

<INPUT type="text" size="20" name="URL">

</FORM>
```

The name attribute used with each form element is important: It assigns a name to the data that is being collected by each text box, button, and any other element you create. The CGI script can then process each bit of data using the name you assign.

Notice that we made the size of all the text-entry boxes the same — 20 characters wide — for consistency. Keep in mind that we didn't set a maxlength value for the boxes, so users can enter as much information as they want, even if the number of characters exceeds 20.

5. Save the file.

6. Display the Web page in your browser. Figure 7-1 shows the result.

Figure 7-1: Using text boxes.

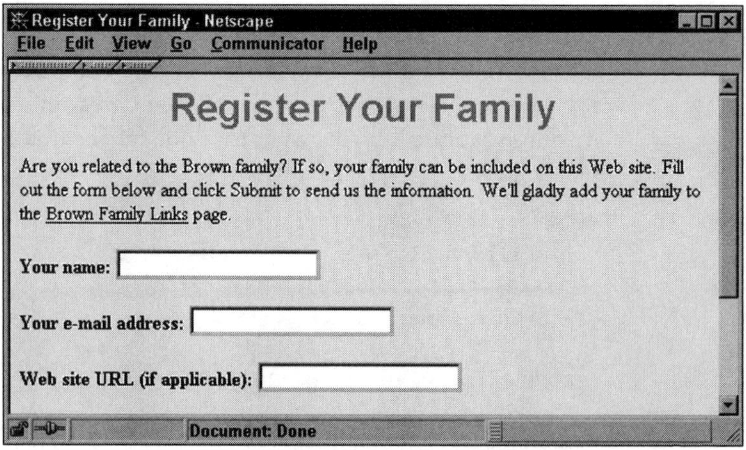

![Screenshot of a Netscape browser window titled "Register Your Family". The page contains a heading "Register Your Family" and text: "Are you related to the Brown family? If so, your family can be included on this Web site. Fill out the form below and click Submit to send us the information. We'll gladly add your family to the Brown Family Links page." Below are three labeled text boxes: "Your name:", "Your e-mail address:", and "Web site URL (if applicable):". The status bar reads "Document: Done".]

Using radio buttons and check boxes

In addition to short, simple text entries, you often want users to be able to choose from a set of options. One way to do this is with the radio and check box types, which create radio buttons or check boxes next to a series of options. The two types work in much the same way, although their appearance is different. Radio buttons are hollow circles that fill in when selected, while check boxes are hollow squares that display a check mark when selected.

The major difference between the two is that check boxes are totally independent of one another. Each has its own name, and any or all of them can be checked at one time. Radio buttons, however, are grouped together by the same name. Selecting one radio button in a group automatically deselects all the others. Of course, you can have several different groups of radio buttons, each group distinguished from the other groups by its distinctive name.

Unlike text boxes, check boxes and radio buttons have definite, preassigned values that a user can't alter, so selecting one always sends the same information. By adding the `checked` attribute, radio buttons or check boxes can be preselected, without any action from the user. In order to change the selection, the user must make a different selection.

To create radio buttons, you repeat the `<INPUT type="radio">` tag for as many buttons as you want. To create check boxes, you repeat `<INPUT type="checkbox">`. Then you add whatever text you want for each option after the tag. On the Register Your Family Page, you can add a set of each of these elements (radio buttons and check boxes) by entering the following code:

```
<P><B>Number of members in your immediate
family:</B>
```

```
<INPUT type="radio" name="members"
value="onetofive">1-5
<INPUT type="radio" name="members"
value="fivetoten">5-10
<INPUT type="radio" name="members"
value="overten">More than 10

<P><B>I am related to:</B>
<INPUT type="checkbox" name="Brownrelation">Brown
family
<INPUT type="checkbox" name="Jonesrelation">Jones
family
<INPUT type="checkbox" name="Smithrelation">Smith
family
<INPUT type="checkbox" name="Doerelation">Doe
family
```

Figure 7-2 shows the result.

Figure 7-2: Using radio buttons and check boxes.

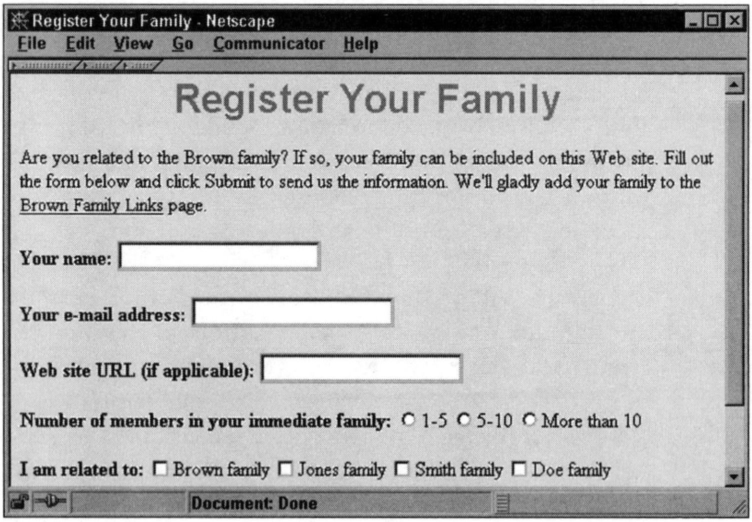

Adding Submit and Reset buttons

Two kinds of buttons are commonly used in forms — Reset and Submit. These buttons have specific functions already built in. If a user clicks a Reset button, all the entries in the form are cleared; the user can then start over. The Submit button, on the other hand, is the one that actually triggers form processing and launches the specified action. You usually see these two buttons at the bottom of a form.

The Reset and Submit buttons use the `<INPUT type="reset">` and `<INPUT type="submit">` tags, respectively. To add these buttons to a forms page, add the following code just before the `</FORM>` end tag:

```
<P><INPUT type="submit" name="submit"
value="Submit">
<INPUT type="reset" name="reset" value="Reset">
```

Figure 7-3 shows the result on the Register Your Family page.

Figure 7-3:   Adding Reset and Submit buttons.

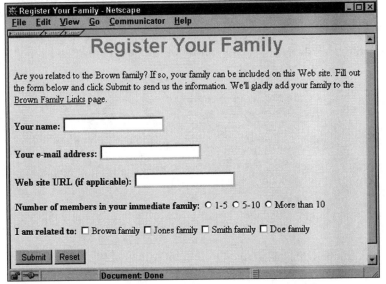

Using the TEXTAREA Element

Sometimes, you may need to get a lot of information from users — more than can fit in a simple text box. So the TEXTAREA element comes into play. Like text boxes, a TEXTAREA element is assigned a name but takes no assigned value, because the value comes from whatever text the user enters.

A TEXTAREA element is quite a bit larger than a text box, though. You set the exact size via the cols (columns, or number of characters per line) and rows (number of lines in the text area) attributes.

The end tag </TEXTAREA> is required. If you wish, you can enter text between the start and end tags; this text then shows up on the form and can be deleted or typed over by the user.

In the Register Your Family page, add a TEXTAREA box so that relatives can submit comments and suggestions to you. To do so, enter the following code after the check boxes you created previously and before the Reset and Submit buttons:

```
<P><B>Feel free to send us some comments or
suggestions for features you'd like to see on
this Web site:</B>
<BR>
<TEXTAREA name="comments" cols="50"
rows="10">Type your text here.</TEXTAREA>
```

The resulting large text box — big enough to let someone send a nice, friendly message — appears in Figure 7-4:

Figure 7-4: Adding a TEXTAREA box.

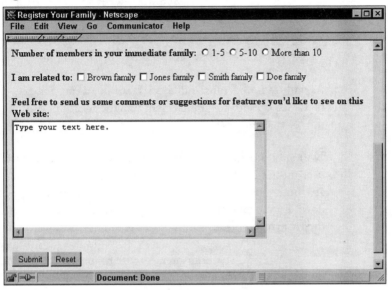

Using the SELECT and OPTION Elements

To present choices in a compact manner, you can hardly beat a drop-down list of options. The amount of space taken up is minimal, yet the number of choices can be tremendous. The only time the list of options intrudes upon the form is during the time the user clicks the list and all the choices appear.

You can use the SELECT element to present a list of choices, each one composed of a single OPTION element.

The OPTION element offers a kind of hybrid approach between the two methods of assigning a value. You can just let the content of the element become the value when it's selected, or you can assign it specifically via the optional value attribute. This method gives you the opportunity to present a more wordy option to the user while keeping the actual data input short and simple. For example, in the following code, the value of the first option is Brown, while the value of the second option is Smith.

```
<OPTION>Brown
<OPTION value=Smith">Smythe or Smith
```

As with radio buttons and check boxes, you can preselect a particular option, but this element uses the `selected` attribute for that purpose.

Normally, the drop-down list shows only the first option; the user must click the list to see the other options. The `size` attribute changes this situation. For example, if the drop-down list contains five options and you set the size to 3, then the first three options show.

The `multiple` attribute alters a more fundamental characteristic — this attribute enables the user to choose more than one option from the same selection list.

Here's how to add a drop-down list to a forms page. In the running example, add an option that enables users to choose the age range they fall into. Just follow these steps:

1. Just below the e-mail address box on the Register Your Family page, type the following code:

```
<P><B>I am in the following age range:</B>
<SELECT name="pickone">
<OPTION>age 10 to 20
<OPTION>age 20 to 40
<OPTION>age 40 to 60
<OPTION>age 60-plus
</SELECT>
```

2. Save the file.

3. Display the Web page in your browser. When you click the arrow next to the drop-down list box (see Figure 7-5), you see the options you've created.

Figure 7-5:   Selection lists.

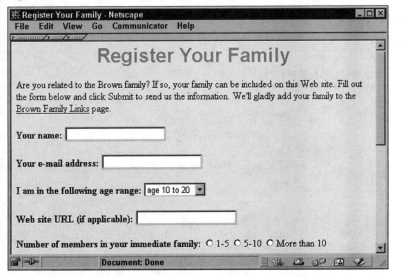

Forms give your Web site's visitors a way to interact with your Web pages and provide you with information. To be extra-considerate of your visitors, you can organize your Web pages using frames that link one page to another and make your site easier to navigate, as described in the next chapter.

CHAPTER 8

BRINGING IT ALL TOGETHER WITH FRAMES

IN THIS CHAPTER

- Understanding framesets
- Using navigation frames
- Targeting frames with hyperlinks
- Adding content for no-frames browsers

By using frames, you can divide up a browser window into two or more panes, each pane holding a different Web page. Frames add interactivity and help readers easily access the contents of multiple Web pages. Frames have long been a favorite tool of Web designers, but use them with care. Many framed pages on the Web are badly designed — some so badly that they're practically useless.

Use frames only when they can improve the functionality of your site. Because each frame holds a separate Web page, the initial download takes a bit more time than a single Web page. Also, make sure that the content of each frame is the right size for it. Many people use frames to cram so much information onto one screen that practically none of the information is viewable without constantly scrolling both vertically and horizontally.

When using frames, bear in mind this rule: Keep it simple — and keep it working.

Understanding Framesets

A *frameset* is not a regular Web page. Rather, a frameset is a Web page that acts as a container for other Web pages that go into individual panes or frames. The frameset identifies the frames and describes their overall arrangement.

Frameset pages don't have a BODY element. Instead, a FRAMESET element goes in place of the BODY element. Within the FRAMESET element, different FRAME elements define areas of the screen to be occupied by conventional Web pages.

Framesets contain no material that is visible in a Web browser, but their TITLE element's content shows up in the title bar of the browser.

Planning frame layout

Framesets tell a Web browser how to divide up its window into individual rows and columns. The `rows` and `cols` attributes of the FRAMESET element specify how many frames are in the browser window. Setting two rows, for instance, divides the window into two horizontal frames:

```
<FRAMESET rows="50%,50%">
<FRAME src="top.htm">
<FRAME src="bottom.htm">
</FRAMESET>
```

Similarly, setting three columns divides the window into three vertical frames:

```
<FRAMESET cols="33%,33%,34%">
<FRAME src="left.htm">
<FRAME src="middle.htm">
<FRAME src="right.htm">
</FRAMESET>
```

Figures 8-1 and 8-2 show what these framesets look like.

Figure 8-1: Dividing a Web page into two horizontal frames.

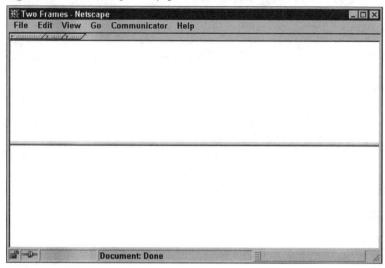

Figure 8-2: Dividing a Web page into three columns.

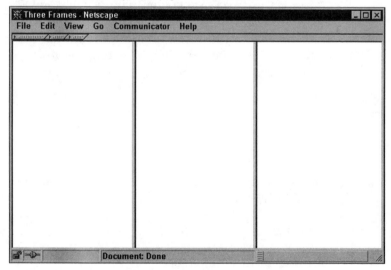

The preceding examples are very simple, stripped-down frames. As you see later in this chapter, each frameset can have columns as well as rows, and each frame/Web page can have its own name and other attributes.

Dividing framesets into rows and columns

The value of the `rows` and `cols` attributes can be one of three kinds — a specific value in pixels, a percentage of the window width, or a relative amount. For example, you can set a columnar format to be two columns, each 100 pixels wide, with the following code:

```
cols="100,100"
```

To set two rows, where the upper row takes up a quarter of the window, you could say:

```
rows="25%,75%"
```

You can accomplish the same thing with a relative value like this:

```
rows="25%,*"
```

The asterisk as the value for the second row means "take up all the available space." Another variation on that approach lets the Web browser work out all the details. In this approach, you simply specify the proportions you want. Thus, to set up four columns with the inner pair twice the size of the outer pair, you use this code:

```
cols="1*,2*,2*,1*"
```

You can simultaneously set both attributes for one frameset. To create a window evenly divided into four sections, for instance, you can use the following code:

```
rows="50%,50%" cols="50%,50%"
```

Adding content

Of course, a frameset is of no value unless you put Web pages in each frame. To add content, you use the FRAME element and its `src` attribute. The value of that attribute is the URL of the Web page that you want to fill the frame.

You need to make sure that the number of frames matches the number of FRAME elements. If you create more frames than you do FRAME elements to fill them, you end up with empty frames.

Internet Explorer doesn't display empty frames, but Netscape Navigator does.

If you've been replicating this book's running example, you can put that content to use in creating your own frames. The frameset you create determines how those frames are arranged and identifies their contents by their Web page names. To create a frameset, use your three Web pages and follow these steps:

1. Open your text editor and create a new document.

2. Save the document with the name framelinks.htm. This is a navigation page that you flesh out with content later in this chapter. Be sure to save the file in the same directory that holds the other documents for your Web site.

3. Create another new document. This one serves as your frameset.

4. Type the following code:

```
<HTML>

<HEAD>
<TITLE>The Brown Family Web Site</TITLE>
</HEAD>
```

```
<FRAMESET cols="20%,80%">
<FRAME name="navigation" src="framelinks.htm">
<FRAME name="content" src="main.htm">
</FRAMESET>

</HTML>
```

The first frame — the navigation frame — is for the framelinks.htm document that you created in Step 1. This document will serve as a table of contents for your Web site. Whenever a visitor clicks a link in the navigation frame, that page appears in the second frame — the content frame. The navigation frame always displays the framelinks.htm document, so visitors always have access to your site's table of contents.

The preceding code specifies the main.htm document (the introductory page for the Brown Family Home Page) as the page that first appears when a visitor enters the URL for the site.

5. Save the file with the name index.htm in the same directory that holds all your Web pages.

Most Web servers have the filename index.htm or index.html set as the default page. For example, if you type the URL www.netwelcome.com, your browser displays the default document index.html, as if you'd typed in the full URL www.netwelcome.com/index.html. Check with your Web host to make sure the default name is index.htm or index.html. If it isn't, then substitute the actual name for index.htm above.

6. Display the index.htm file in your browser (see Figure 8-3). Don't worry that the left frame (which is assigned 20 percent of the Web page's width) is blank. The important thing to notice, for now, is that the right frame (which is assigned the remaining 80 percent of the page width) is your Brown Family Home Page.

Figure 8-3: Two frames.

Exploring frames options

In addition to the `src` attribute, FRAME elements also have several other attributes. We tell you about the `target` attribute later in the section called "Using targets." For now, take a look at the other attributes of this element:

■ The `scrolling` attribute controls whether visitors can use scroll bars in cases where the frame's content exceeds its size. Most people don't use this attribute, allowing the browser to decide. You can, however, set it to values of yes, no, or auto (which is the default value — the same as not using the attribute at all). Yes means that scroll bars always appear, whether they're needed or not; no means that scroll bars never appear, even if the content exceeds the size of the frame.

■ The `noresize` attribute overrides the users' ability to make a frame larger or smaller by dragging the frame borders to a new location. This attribute takes no value and should be used only when the exact dimensions of the layout are absolutely critical. Many different screen resolutions are used on the Web, and some users may have to rearrange the frames in order to be able to see them properly.

■ The `frameborder` attribute can be set to a value of either 0 or 1. These values are a throwback to the early days of programming, when "0" meant "no" and "1" meant "yes." So, setting `frameborder="0"` means that the frame won't have a border. Setting it to 1 doesn't mean much, because borders appear by default. Eliminating frame borders is a chancy thing to manage, because any frame that abuts the borderless frame has its own border. You need to remove the borders from every abutting frame in order to see any effect.

■ The `marginheight` and `marginwidth` attributes are much like the cell padding in tables (see Chapter 6). They increase the distance between the frame's contents and its border. They take an absolute value in pixels.

Take care when using these attributes. Setting frames so that they have no border, for instance, can look pretty weird if some of the frames require scroll bars. Altering margin height and width can also cause the contents of frames, such as tables, to change their dimensions to meet the new requirements.

To see the effect of setting no borders, you could change the HTML for the two frames in your frameset to the following:

```
<FRAME src="framelinks.htm" frameborder="0">
<FRAME src="main.htm" frameborder="0">
```

If you saved this HTML and opened the resulting page in your browser, you would notice that the border between the frames had disappeared. But for this example, leave the border in and proceed to the next stage: creating a navigational page.

Using Navigation Frames

One of the most common uses of frames is for navigation. One frame retains its original content so visitors can click its links and thereby alter the content of another frame.

Generally speaking, the navigation frame is much smaller than the main, or content, frame. Sometimes, the design places the navigation frame on the top or the left side. Much less often, it may be placed on the right or at the bottom of the screen. In the frameset you created earlier in this chapter, this arrangement of the two frames is already set up. The navigation frame (which was assigned a name with the attribute name="navigation") takes up 20 percent of the Web page width, while the content frame (which was assigned a name with the attribute name="content") takes up the remainder.

The purpose of the navigation frame is to provide links to all the pages in the three-page example Web site: main.htm, links.htm, and register.htm. That way, no matter what page appears in the content frame, the viewer can click a link in the navigation frame to cause a different linked page to appear in the content frame. To set up this navigation frame, follow these steps:

1. Open framelinks.htm in your text editor.

2. Type the following code:

```
<HTML>

<HEAD>
<TITLE>The Brown Family Web Site</TITLE>
</HEAD>

<BODY bgcolor="beige">

<P><A href="main.htm">The Brown Family Home
```

```
Page</A>
<P><A href="links.htm">Brown Family Links</A>
<P><A href="register.htm">Register Your
Family</A>

</BODY>
</HTML>
```

3. Save the file.

4. Open the index.htm page in your Web browser (or, if
the index.htm frameset page is still showing in your
browser, reload or refresh the page to update its contents). The results are shown in Figure 8-4.

Figure 8-4:   A navigation frame contains links to the important pages on a Web site.

Using targets

Frames really get interactive when you click a link in one
frame and the page that corresponds to that link appears in
another frame. This situation is where the names that are

assigned to frames come in: When you make a link in one page, you can assign that link a target frame with the `tar-get` attribute in the FRAME element. When the user clicks on the link, the page appears in the frame that is named as a value to the `target` attribute. The code follows this form:

```
<FRAME src="pagename.htm" target="framename">
```

On the frameset you created earlier in this chapter, you named the navigation frame "navigation" and the content frame "content." By using the `target` attribute with the value "content," you can make each link in the navigation frame cause the appropriate Web page to be loaded into the content frame. Here's what the resulting code looks like:

```
<P><A href="main.htm" target="content">The Brown
Family Home Page</A>
<P><A href="links.htm" target="content">Brown
Family Links</A>
<P><A href="register.htm"
target="content">Register Your Family</A>
```

Adding NOFRAMES content

Some Web browsers still don't support frames. For those browsers, you may want to add some sort of information that lets visitors know why they're not seeing what you intended. You can do this via the NOFRAMES element, which should be the last thing before the FRAMESET's end tag. When you add the NOFRAMES content to the index.htm document, the resulting code looks like this:

```
<FRAMESET cols="20%,80%">
<FRAME name="navigation" src="framelinks.htm">
<FRAME name="content" src="main.htm">
<NOFRAMES>
<P>This page shows two frames. Without a frames-
capable Web browser, you won't be able to see the
```

```
page.</P>
</NOFRAMES>
</FRAMESET>
```

When you add NOFRAMES content and open your page in your Web browser, you don't actually see anything because your browser does display frames. The NOFRAMES information is only for those viewers whose browsers don't show frames: Those users see only the NOFRAMES content, not the frames or their contents.

If you want to see NOFRAMES content in action, download a bare-bones Web browser, such as Lynx, that does not support frames. You can find a huge list of Web browsers, including Lynx, that you can download at the BrowserWatch Web site (`http://browserwatch.internet.com/browsers.html`).

CHAPTER 9

MOVING FORWARD WITH YOUR WEB SITE

IN THIS CHAPTER

- Reviewing your Web pages before you publish
- Finding a Web host and Web publishing software
- Checking and revising your Web pages

Creating your Web site is just the initial step. Managing your site is an ongoing process that includes publishing and revising your Web pages. By *publishing* your pages, you move them from your computer to a special computer called a *Web server*. A Web server is a computer that is connected to the Internet 24 hours a day, seven days a week, and can serve Web pages to anyone who requests them by entering the proper URL.

In this chapter, we provide tips on checking your site before you publish it, finding a place for it on the Internet, and keeping your Web pages up-to-date.

Checking Your Pages

Before you publish your Web pages, check them one more time before they go public. Open each page and look at it in a Web browser, just as your visitors are going to do. Be sure to check your pages in both of the major browsers — Netscape Navigator and Microsoft Internet Explorer. Then do the following:

■ **Read your words.** Remember, your pages are going to be visible to strangers as well as your nearest and dearest. Be sure to read the text (or have a friend do so) and catch any misspellings.

■ **Check your links.** Click each hypertext link and make sure it does what it's supposed to do.

■ **Test your graphics.** Make sure your images appear on your pages where you want them to. Sometimes, images don't appear because you didn't correctly enter the path to them using the IMG element or because you forgot one or both of the quotation marks around the image's filename.

Catching mistakes up-front really pays off. Would you rather have a stranger or a relative point out "boo-boos" that make you look bad? We didn't think so.

Putting Your Pages Online

A painter needs to find an art gallery where people can view his or her artwork. Similarly, after you have an Internet connection and have created Web pages, the next step is to display your pages on the World Wide Web. To do that, here's what you need:

■ **A Web hosting service.** Almost all ISPs include free Web server space as part of their Internet access. If your ISP does this, then you're set; just follow your ISP's directions for placing Web pages on its server. If not, you may want to shop for a Web hosting service. Table 9-1 provides a few suggestions. Your Web hosting service can provide you with all the information you need to upload your pages to the Internet.

Table 9-1 Web Hosting Services

Web Host	URL	Comments
Yahoo! GeoCities	www.geocities.com	This popular site lets you publish Web pages for free; you can get a free e-mail address, too.
XOOM.com	xoom.com	Besides Web publishing space, you get free software and access to chat rooms where you can meet other Web site authors.
Tripod	www.tripod.com	Members can publish pages as well as chat and post messages on message boards.
AOL Hometown	hometown.aol.com	This is America Online's free Web hosting site on the Internet.

■ **File transfer software.** To move your Web page files from your computer to a Web server (the techie term is *upload*), you need a program to transfer the files. The kind of software you need depends on your Web host. Most Web hosts support a type of Internet communication called *File Transfer Protocol* (*FTP*). A common — and free! — FTP program for Windows is WS_FTP Lite, which you can download from www.ipswitch.com. If you use a Macintosh, you can download the FTP program Fetch from www.dartmouth.edu/pages/softdev/fetch.html.

You may already have free Web publishing software on your own PC. Windows 98 provides you with a built-in publishing tool called Web Publishing Wizard. If you use Windows 95, you can get WPW as part of the Microsoft Internet Explorer package, which you can download for free from www.microsoft.com/ie.

For more information on publishing your pages, see the CliffsNotes Resource Center at the back of this book.

Visiting Your New Web Site

One of the most exciting aspects of creating Web pages is when you enter the URL given to you by your Web host and visit your new Web site for the first time. You need to enter the same URL your visitors use. That way, you can make sure the URL works correctly. Such a URL may resemble the following:

```
http://www.webhost.com/~username/
```

The tilde symbol (~) often identifies a user's directory on a Web server.

If the URL is correct and all your files were transferred, your home page should appear.

Revising Your Web Pages

After you get your pages online, the real fun begins. Tell your friends and family to visit your site and give you feedback. Listen to their suggestions and revise your site.

Revisions are important because they keep your information up-to-date. To make changes easily (and to ensure that you have a backup copy of your files, just in case something happens to your Web server), keep a copy of all your HTML files and images on your computer. Make revisions on your own machine and then publish the updated files, replacing the outdated files on the Web server with the updated ones on your computer. Then your friends and relatives, as well as the public at large, can admire your hard work!

CLIFFSNOTES REVIEW

Use this CliffsNotes Review to practice what you've learned in this book and to build your confidence in doing the job right the first time. After you work through the review questions, the problem-solving exercises, and the fun and useful practice projects, you're well on your way to achieving your goal of creating your own Web pages with HTML.

Q&A

1. Which element holds the viewable content of a Web page?
   a. TITLE
   b. BODY
   c. HEAD

2. Name the three major font families. _____
   _____

3. What does CGI stand for?
   a. Complete Gateway Interface
   b. Common Gateway Internet
   c. Common Gateway Interface

4. Where does the BODY element go in a frameset?
   a. Within the TITLE element
   b. Nowhere
   c. In the first frame

5. When should you use the `noresize` attribute with frames?
   _____

6. Which of the following elements can tables hold?
   a. IMG
   b. TABLE
   c. H2

7. What is the main advantage of the CENTER element?

   a. It simultaneously aligns all the elements contained within it.

   b. It has a greater number of alignment options than other elements.

   c. It can vertically align other elements.

8. How does an absolute URL differ from a relative URL?

   a. The absolute URL does not include a filename.

   b. The absolute URL does not use directory names.

   c. The absolute URL begins with `http://` or another type of Internet protocol.

Answers: (1) b. (2) Monospace, serif, and sans serif. (3) c. (4) b. (5) When it's absolutely imperative that the size of the frames not be altered by a user. (6) All of them. (7) a. (8) c.

Scenarios

1. You want to use a background image that will tile evenly into the following common screen widths: 640, 800, 1024. You should _____.

2. You've created more frames than FRAME elements in a frameset, resulting in some empty frames. You should_____ _____.

3. You add a horizontal rule to your Web page, not setting any attributes. When you view it in different browsers, you see that the thickness varies. You should _____ _____.

4. You outgrow your ISP's Web page space allowances and decide to move your site to a new URL. You should _____ _____.

Answers: (1) Pick one with a width of a common denominator like 32. (2) Either delete one of the frames or add a FRAME element to hold it. (3) Set a specific value for the `size` attribute. (4) Set up a redirection page at your old URL.

Consider This

■ Did you know that you can use a frameset as the content of a frame? Just set the src attribute of a FRAME element to the URL of another frameset. See Chapter 8 for more information on frames.

■ Did you know that people can set their Web browsers to not print the background color of a Web page? This means that, if you use a dark background color with light text, users may not be able to see the text on a printout. See Chapter 2 for information on background color.

Practice Project

1. Make a Web page that lists all the named colors and set each color name to that color. For example:

```
<P><FONT color="aliceblue">aliceblue</FONT>
<P><FONT color="antiquewhite">antiquewhite</FONT>
<P><FONT color="aqua">aqua</FONT>
<P><FONT color="aquamarine">aquamarine</FONT>
```

See Chapter 2 for more information.

2. See what happens if you apply the FONT element to some characters in an H1 element. Can you change their size? See Chapter 2 for more information.

3. See how many BLOCKQUOTE elements you can nest before you end up with only one word per line. See Chapter 3 for more information.

CLIFFSNOTES RESOURCE CENTER

The learning doesn't need to stop here. CliffsNotes Resource Center shows you the best of the best — links to the best information in print and online about HTML. Look for all the terrific resources at your favorite bookstore or local library and on the Internet. When you're online, make your first stop www.cliffsnotes.com, where you can find more incredibly useful information about HTML.

Books

This CliffsNotes book is one of many great books about HTML and Web page design published by IDG Books Worldwide, Inc. So if you want some great next-step books, check out these other publications:

Creating Web Pages, 4th Edition, by Bud Smith and Arthur Bebak. This book introduces you to the ins and outs of publishing on the Web, including putting your pages on WebTV. IDG Books Worldwide, Inc., $24.99.

Dynamic HTML For Dummies, 2nd Edition, by Michael Hyman. Expand your existing Web pages by adding dazzling multimedia and Cascading Style Sheets. IDG Books Worldwide, Inc., $29.99.

HTML 4 For Dummies, 2nd Edition, by Ed Tittel and Natanya Pitts. This reference presents the plain-English fundamentals of writing HTML for the World Wide Web. You can also find definitions for every HTML tag imaginable. IDG Books Worldwide, Inc., $29.99.

HTML Publishing Bible, by Alan Simpson. The ultimate reference/tutorial for HTML, written by bestselling author Alan Simpson. IDG Books Worldwide, Inc., $39.99.

Teach Yourself HTML 4, by Stephanie Cottrell Bryant. Are you a visual person? Then, this is the book for you. Tons of illustrations help you expand your HTML knowledge. Advanced topics include editing images, creating CGI scripts, and working in XML (the parent markup language of HTML). IDG Books Worldwide, Inc., $29.99.

You can easily find books published by IDG Books Worldwide, Inc., in your favorite bookstores, at the library, on the Internet, and at a store near you. We also have three Web sites that you can use to read about all the books we publish:

- www.cliffsnotes.com

- www.dummies.com

- www.idgbooks.com

Internet

Check out these Web sites for more information about HTML and Web page design:

Addicted to Graphics by Brenda Kay, www.design-heaven.com/users/brendakay/home.html, offers clip art images that you can download.

Browser Caps, www.browsercaps.com/config/Sv/, keeps track of which Web browsers support which features of the HTML standard.

Browser Watch, http://browserwatch.internet.com, keeps you up-to-date on the latest news about Web browsers and plug-ins.

CGI Resource Index, www.cgi-resources.com, is a great source of CGI programs.

Clipart4Free, www.clipart4free.com, lets you download tons of clip art images for free.

Color Names and R-G-B Values, www.interlinked.com/color-chart.html, lists the HTML color names and provides examples of how the colors look.

Compendium of HTML Elements, www.htmlcompendium.org/index.htm, is one of the premier locations on the World Wide Web for learning about HTML. Look up detailed information on any element.

FormSite.com, www.formsite.com, is where you can create a form online that has a built-in CGI script to process the data you receive.

FreeCode, www.freecode.com/index.html, provides plenty of free CGI programs for your use.

HTML Writers Guild, www.hwg.org, is a group dedicated to promoting good Web page authorship.

Matt's Script Archive, http://worldwidemart.com/scripts/, is a venerable and well-known source for CGI programs.

Project Cool Developer Zone, www.projectcool.com/developer/, is where you find discussion groups, design tips, information on Cascading Style Sheets, JavaScript, audio, and much more.

Web Developer's Virtual Library, www.stars.com, is a prime resource, including info on Perl, Dynamic HTML, multimedia on the Web, and some great tutorials.

Winfiles.com Windows 95/98 HTML Color Pickers, www.winfiles.com/apps/98/colorpick.html, is where you can find all sorts of programs that help you choose the colors for your Web pages.

World Wide Web Consortium, www.w3.org/TR/WD-html40/, is the home of the official HTML specification.

Yale C/AIM Web Style Guide, http://info.med.yale.edu/caim/manual/, gives recommendations for creating Web page content.

Next time you're on the Internet, don't forget to drop by www.cliffsnotes.com. We created an online Resource Center that you can use today, tomorrow, and beyond.

Send Us Your Favorite Tips

In your quest for learning, have you ever experienced that sublime moment when you figure out a trick that saves time or trouble? Perhaps you realized you were taking ten steps to accomplish something that could take two. Or you found a little-known workaround that gets great results. If you've discovered a useful tip that helped you use HTML more effectively and you'd like to share it, the CliffsNotes staff would love to hear from you. Go to our Web site at www.cliffsnotes.com and click the Talk to Us button. If we select your tip, we may publish it as part of *CliffsNotes Daily*, our exciting, free e-mail newsletter. To find out more or to subscribe to the newsletter, go to www.cliffsnotes.com on the Web.

INDEX

~ (tilde) user directory prefix, 111
"" (quotation marks) attribute delimiters, 10
& (ampersand) character code prefix, 31
  (nonbreaking space), 16, 73
; (semicolon) character code suffix, 31
< > (angle brackets) tag delimiters, 9
= (equal sign) attribute prefix, 10

A

A element, 58
action attribute, 84
align attribute
  described, 32
  horizontal rules, 37, 40
  images, 52
  table cells, 76
alignment
  images, 52–53
  tables, 69, 75, 76–77
  text, 32–37
alink attribute, 63
alt attribute, 49
anchors, 58
AOL Hometown Web site, 110
attributes, 10–12. *See also* names of specific attributes

B

B element, 23–24
background attribute, 53
background color, 21
background images, 45, 53–55
bgcolor attribute, 21
blank spaces, 11, 16, 73
BLOCKQUOTE element, 35–36
BODY element, 9–10, 21, 53
bold text, 23–24
border attribute, 48
BR element, 16, 34
BrowserWatch Web site, 107

C

CAPTION element, 67–68, 70
Cascading Style Sheets (CSS), 25
case sensitivity, 12
cellpadding attribute, 78
cellspacing attribute, 78
CENTER element, 37
centering text, 33, 37
CGI (Common Gateway Interface), 83–84
check boxes, 89–90

checked attribute, 89
CliffsNotes Web site, 45
color
  background, 21
  links, 63
  text, 20–23
color pickers, 21
cols attribute, 92, 97, 99
Common Gateway Interface (CGI), 83–84
container relationship, 9–10
copyright, 45
CSS (Cascading Style Sheets), 25

E

elements. *See also* names of specific elements
  alignment, 32–37
  block-level, 12
  combining, 13
  container relationship, 9–10
  described, 8
  inline, 12, 23–24
  notation convention, 12
e-mail links, 64–65

F

Fetch (file transfer software), 110
File Transfer Protocol (FTP), 110
file transfer software, 110
font
  bold, 23–24
  color, 20–23
  face, 26–28
  italics, 23–24
  monospace, 27
  serif/sans serif, 26
  size, 25–26, 31
  special characters, 28–31
  strikethrough, 23
  underlined, 23
  Web browser substitution, 27
FONT element, 21, 27
FORM element, 84
forms
  CGI script processing, 83–84
  check boxes, 89–90
  creating, 84
  design issues, 83
  preset choices, 93–95
  radio buttons, 89–90
  reset buttons, 91
  submit buttons, 91
  text boxes, 85–88, 92–93
frameborder attribute, 103

CliffsNotes™

Your shortcut to
success™
for over 40 years

Computers and Software
Confused by computers? Struggling with software? Let
CliffsNotes get you up to speed on the fundamentals —
quickly and easily. Titles include:

Balancing Your Checkbook with Quicken®
Buying Your First PC
Creating a Dynamite PowerPoint® 2000 Presentation
Making Windows® 98 Work for You
Setting up a Windows® 98 Home Network
Upgrading and Repairing Your PC
Using Your First PC
Using Your First iMac™
Writing Your First Computer Program

The Internet
Intrigued by the Internet? Puzzled about life online?
Let *CliffsNotes* show you how to get started with e-mail,
Web surfing, and more. Titles include:

Buying and Selling on eBay®
Creating Web Pages with HTML
Creating Your First Web Page
Exploring the Internet with Yahoo!®
Finding a Job on the Web
Getting on the Internet
Going Online with AOL®
Shopping Online Safely